David Hume

SUNY series in Contemporary Continental Philosophy

Dennis J. Schmidt, editor

David Hume

Platonic Philosopher, Continental Ancestor

BERNARD FREYDBERG

Cover art: *Vews of the Bosphorus*, drawings by Akiko Kotani.

Published by State University of New York Press, Albany

© 2012 State University of New York

All rights reserved

Printed in the United States of America

No part of this book may be used or reproduced in any manner whatsoever without written permission. No part of this book may be stored in a retrieval system or transmitted in any form or by any means including electronic, electrostatic, magnetic tape, mechanical, photocopying, recording, or otherwise without the prior permission in writing of the publisher.

For information, contact State University of New York Press, Albany, NY
www.sunypress.edu

Production by Ryan Morris
Marketing by Kate McDonnell

Library of Congress Cataloging-in-Publication Data

Freydberg, Bernard, 1947–
  David Hume : platonic philosopher, continental ancestor / Bernard Freydberg.
    p. cm. — (SUNY series in contemporary continental philosophy)
  Includes bibliographical references and index.
  ISBN 978-1-4384-4215-0 (hardcover : alk. paper)
  ISBN 978-1-4384-4214-3 (pbk. : alk. paper)
  1. Hume, David, 1711–1776. I. Title.

B1498.F74 2012
192—dc23   2011023763

10 9 8 7 6 5 4 3 2 1

For Dennis J Schmidt:
Original Thinker, Friend to Philosophy and Philosophers

Contents

Acknowledgments	ix
Introduction	1
Deleuze's Hume . . . and Ours: Madness, Retrieval	9
Chapter I Aspects of *An Enquiry Concerning Human Understanding*	17
Chapter II Aspects of *An Enquiry Concerning the Principles of Morals*	49
Chapter III Hume's Philosophy of Art	93
Conclusion	113
Notes	119
Bibliography	129
Index	133

Acknowledgments

The following people and institutions supported the writing of this book in various ways. I thank them, one and all, more than I can say.

I was blessed with two terrific editors at the State University of New York Press. Jane Bunker, Editor in Chief, with whom I began this book before she moved on to the directorship at Northwestern University Press, is a brilliant editor and a brilliant human being. Given her background in philosophy, her support for this book gave me much confidence. Andrew Kenyon, now Assistant Acquisitions Editor and in charge of philosophy books, has been a delight to work with.

Sami Gülgöz, Dean of the School of Social Sciences and Humanities at Koç University, Istanbul, approved a leave for the summer of 2008 that made the research and part of the writing of this book possible. Shannon Sullivan, Chair of the Pennsylvania State University Philosophy Department, granted me the position of Visiting Scholar for that same summer. This enabled me to avail myself of the wonderful Penn State libraries and other facilities. James Swindal, Chair of the Duquesne University Philosophy Department, graciously appointed me Scholar in Residence, the post I now occupy. I completed the book under his and its aegis.

Two anonymous readers for the State University of New York Press provided me with reviews that combined encouragement with astute criticism. A long conversation with Jennifer Mensch of the Penn State Philosophy Department on pre-Kantian philosophy was most illuminating. Michael Rudar and John Fritz, two of my former undergraduate philosophy students who are completing their PhD degrees at Duquesne University, proofread and offered helpful comments on the manuscript. Both will surely be excellent professors before too long.

Kathleen Manning and Rita McClelland of Bailey Library at Slippery Rock University were, as they have been in the past, exceptionally helpful in securing materials for this book. One could not hope for better librarians.

My wife, Akiko Kotani, inspires me in every way. Once again, her view as an artist on imagination has influenced my own, and she is a marvelous partner in all that I attempt. My daughter, Malika Hadley Freydberg, also gives me wings by virtue of her intelligence and great spirit.

Dennis J. Schmidt has made important contributions to philosophy on every level. His scholarly work always breaks new ground. He has regularly had a prominent role in organizing important conferences and events. As a teacher, he presents lectures and conducts that challenge, encourage, and open new pathways for his hearers. As editor of this series, he has overseen the publication of more than one hundred Continental philosophy books over the years. My debt is to him considerable, and it is an honor to be his colleague. With humility and great pleasure, I dedicate this book to him.

Introduction

My ambition for this book is large. With it, I seek to locate David Hume incontestably as a most worthy ancestor of and for Continental philosophy. While his thought receives occasional treatment, especially in Husserl, and while Deleuze's 1953 *Empiricism and Subjectivity: An Essay on Hume's Theory of Human Nature* provides a daring and valuable reading of the *Treatise of Human Nature*,[1] no single book in the Continental tradition (at least to my knowledge) attempts an overview of Hume's philosophy in terms of its major developments in interpretation. Among these, I consider especially Heidegger's of Kant, Merleau-Ponty's of Husserl, and Sallis's of Plato (as well as of many others). These interpretations combine scrupulous regard for the texts with creative excavations yielding heretofore untapped resources. Happy indeed (as Hume would write) if in this book such fine scholarship joins with such worthy novel insights!

I find an inspiration for this task in a well-known turning point in philosophy's history. According to my view, the greatest Hume scholar to date and perhaps forever is Immanuel Kant. In his time, he alone grasped the radicality and the force of his Scottish forbear's thought. After denouncing the obtuse responses of Reid, Oswald, Beatty, and Priestly to Hume, he famously wrote in the *Prolegomena*:

> I openly confess my recollection of *David Hume* was the very thing that many years ago first interrupted my dogmatic slumber and gave my investigations in the field of speculative philosophy a quite new direction.[2]

The word *recollection* is hardly innocent in philosophy. While one cannot make any direct connection between Kantian and Platonic recollection (though Kant knew Greek well, and undoubtedly read Plato in both Greek and German), I venture to assert at least a strong analogy[3]: Along with the voluminous contents in the soul of Kant, there dwelled the arguments of Hume. With suddenness at some point, Kant saw how powerfully his thought challenged both modern rationalism and modern empiricism—just as it challenged his own lifelong efforts as a metaphysician. It is impossible to fix the precise date at which he experienced the full power of Hume's insight, but his Inaugural Dissertation, which still contained traces of rational metaphysics, was delivered in 1777 when he was fifty-three years old, and the *Critique of Pure Reason* first appeared in 1781.

The central Transcendental Deduction took many years and much labor to complete. The framework and the setting of the problem can be found in Kant's 1772 well-known letter to Markus Herz:

> [A]s to how my understanding may form for itself concepts of things completely a priori, with which concepts the things must necessarily agree, and as to how my understanding may formulate real principles concerning the possibility of such concepts, and experience must faithfully agree with these principles which nevertheless are independent of experience—this question, of how the faculty of understanding achieves this conformity with the things themselves, is still left in a state of obscurity.[4]

In his November 14, 1776, letter to Herz, Kant indicated that while he would likely be unable to complete the *Critique* before Easter, he "shall use part of next summer for it."[5] "[P]art of next summer" became four years.

There can be no doubt that Hume hovered over all of Kant's labors, making them more arduous at every turn. Testimony of Hume's influence could not be more compelling given the still lively, penetrating, and spirited interpretations of the Transcendental Deduction (A edition, B edition, and both together). As a lover who's brave enough to take on lost causes and articulate them with skill, I mention Gottfried Martin's 1953 *Immanuel Kant, Ontologie und Wissenschaftstheorie* (translated as *Kant's Metaphysics and Theory of Science*),[6] whose articulation is all the more remarkable as a result of what he does not say. The name Hume appears nowhere in it, making it unique and, to employ an admittedly much overused cliché, establishing the exception that proves the rule. Yet another: Hume is the elephant in the room on every page. If there were no Hume, it is difficult if not impossible to imagine a critical philosophy of Kant.

Although many Hume scholars recognize the importance of imagination to his thought,[7] none to my knowledge read Hume such that the generation of images is the *sine qua non* of his theoretical and practical thought, and that this aspect has primary importance for Kant's response; nor do any regard this aspect as a source for Continental philosophy. My primary purpose is to raise the all-important matter of *imagination,* tracing it from Hume through Kant and farther in the Continental tradition, where it begins to lose its centrality after Schelling for more than a century. In my view, it is the preeminent faculty or function: it generates fictions that can become beliefs, it is the freest device of all, and—more to the point—imagination alone makes possible and empowers the transition between past constant conjunctions to the unavoidable supposition to their continuation in the future, the sole basis of that fiction-become-belief that we call cause and effect.

One could say with justification that it was Hume's analysis of the concept of cause and effect, treating it as is fundamentally fictional,[8] that jolted Kant awake. But this means that the curious "new impression" produced by imagination after repeated conjunctions must also figure in his arousal. In my view, it is not too much to claim that the single most distinctive contribution to philosophy of Kant's thought is the notion of a *productive imagination.*[9] Though the *precise* determination is open to dispute, and though Kant said of himself that he saw farther and more deeply than Hume despite his enormous debt to him, there can be little doubt that Hume's imagination is the forerunner of Kant's in the history of thought.

Johann von Gottlieb Fichte, whose relationship to his implicit master grew gradually more problematic, attempted to systematize the principles of Kantian philosophy in his 1794 *Grundlage der gesamte Wissenschftslehre (Foundation of the Doctrine of Science).* Whatever the details of their gradual distance, the outcome of the *Grundlage* in its theoretical division places imagination unmistakably and emphatically at the center of human thought:

> All the difficulties that obstructed our path have been resolved. The task was that of uniting the opposites, I and not-I. By the power of imagination *(Einbildungskraft),* which reconciles contradictions, they can be perfectly united.[10]

One could say that for Fichte, imagination always already hovers *(schwebt)* between I and not-I, that is, circles or mediates between Leibnizian and Humean thought. However, one finds no recognition of the role of Hume's thought in the crucial interdetermination that constitutes experience for us.[11]

Friedrich von Josef Schelling takes imagination still farther, elevating it to the divine, cosmic plane. Schelling spaces the word for the divine act of imagination as *E i n-b i l d e n.*[12] The human act *images* the divine act, creatively shaping it into a one. The eternality of divine imagination is reflected in what Schelling earlier calls "the profound logic of the ancients"[13] that nestles the law of sufficient reason within it. It is difficult to determine, however, whether Schelling does more justice to Hume than does Fichte, who virtually ignores him. Schelling writes with some breeziness: "It is strange enough that [Hume's] refutation was found to be so difficult, as no one until now has noticed the very simple fact that it can *even* be refuted by experience."[14] Thus, can we conclude that Kant could have spared himself all of his strenuous labors if only he noticed a "simple fact"? (I say this as a champion of Schelling's thought in general, having devoted much time in writing a book explicating and endorsing his thought.)[15]

Speaking logically, Schelling's argument both affirms the consequent and restates something Hume "never thought of doubting." Schelling maintains that human beings, including the very first one, have employed this concept, so it belongs to human nature. He goes so far as making an appeal to the biblical Fall: when the snake tells Adam what will happen if he eats the fruit, this presupposes that Adam already understands causality. Despite the enormous and necessary influence Hume had on the fashioning of Kant's critical philosophy, a philosophy without which theirs could not have begun, Fichte and Schelling demonstrate no evidence of having studied Hume's philosophy with any seriousness. These two non-encounters mark the beginning of the rapidly increasing neglect of Hume on our Continental side of the tradition to which his thought contributed so much.

Enter Hegel, whose *Lectures on the History of Philosophy* at least include a section on Hume, although at six pages it is less than half the length of the one devoted to Jacobi. Hegel grants no intrinsic value to Hume's thought:

> [Humean skepticism] is more noteworthy historically than it is in itself; its historical noteworthiness consists in this, that Kant properly took up the point of origin of his philosophy from him.[16]

What follows is a superficial account of Hume's treatment of cause and effect which, if presented by an advanced undergraduate, would not satisfy her professor. His ascription of a moral relativism to Hume is, quite simply, mistaken. Small wonder that those of us who seek nourishment from Hegel on philosophy's leading figures do not learn to savor Hume's offerings!

A kinship of sorts between Nietzsche and Hume has been claimed of late, motivated largely by their mutual negative accounts of religion and their general antirationalism. And there is textual evidence that Nietzsche acknowledged and welcomed these qualities in his Scottish predecessor. However, it would be mistaken to claim any more than a minimum role for Hume in Nietzsche's thought, far more of an affinity than of an influence. The mentions of Hume are very scarce, and they never unfold into even brief philosophical analyses. If one seeks a genuine appreciation of Hume's thought one will not find it in Nietzsche's. And one seeks in vain for any but the most cursory mentions of it in Merleau-Ponty, Heidegger, and Derrida.

It is to Husserl's credit that he recognized that Hume's significance extends far beyond his critique of the causal principle. Further, it is clear that he actually *read* Hume, at least the whole of Part I of the *Treatise* and the whole of the first *Enquiry*. In the Encyclopedia Britannica article, Husserl writes:

> Here lies the new task, an all-embracing eidetic phenomenology of association, a later-day rehabilitation of David Hume's great discovery, involving an account of the a priori genesis out of which a real spatial world constitutes itself for the mind in habitual acceptance.[17]

This interpretation of association, while not Hume's, can be seen as flowing from it. One suspects, however, that perhaps "contiguity"—or perhaps contiguity together with association—would be a more apt choice, and may be what Husserl had in mind. As will be shown in the main text, once cause and effect is subtracted from the three relations of ideas on account of its unaccountability, what remains is a clear ancestor to a twentieth-century phenomenological philosophy.

Hume also receives extensive analysis in the first volume of *Logical Investigations* for his discussion of abstraction. Husserl correctly notes Hume's Berkeleyan heritage: unlike Locke, neither Berkeley nor Hume held that ideas could be abstracted entirely from content; an abstract idea always included a *perception* that had been separated off (ab-stracted) from its occurrence in experience. Husserl writes:

> [W]e do not contradict ourselves if, on the one hand, we say that Hume's [radical subjectivism] was an extreme case of error, and yet vindicate it for the glory of having shown the way to a psychological theory of abstraction.[18]

Hume's radical subjectivism, which famously argued against the notion of a unified self apart from its perceptions, leads Husserl to posit a transcendental, intentional subject in terms of which a new transcendental psychology transforms and replaces Humean empiricism.

However, Husserl's thoroughgoing seriousness works against his ultimate Hume interpretation, which—in my view—must also glorify the playfulness that animates it. Husserl writes with unseemly sanctimoniousness:

> Astounding as Hume's genius is, it is the more regrettable that a correspondingly great philosophical ethos is not joined with it. This is evident in the fact that Hume takes care, throughout his whole presentation, blandly to disguise or interpret as harmless his absurd results . . .[19]

He proceeds to criticize Hume for assuming the easy role of an academic skeptic instead of struggling against the absurdities, and so of fathering an unhealthy positivism—demonstrating that even the great and scrupulous Husserl can fall victim to arguments *ad hominem*.

It is high time for Hume's thought to be incorporated into contemporary Continental philosophy where it properly belongs. This means that it must be interpreted according to its best insights, its playfulness must be celebrated, and its conveyance of Socratic ignorance into the modern discourse be justly elaborated. The success of this volume depends entirely upon the degree to which these goals are achieved.

Toward that achievement, this book has been organized to highlight both aspects of the title. As a prelude, Gilles Deleuze's marvelous *Empiricism and Subjectivity: An Essay on Hume's Theory of Human Nature* (1953) serves as entryway to Hume's singular thought as this thought unfolds into contemporary Continental concerns. Deleuze recognizes that Hume's "empiricism" cannot be contained within its own confines, but spirals out of itself into a delirium that resides at the heart of thinking. Madness is certainly no stranger to philosophy; it drives Plato's *Phaedrus* as both one of its main topics as well as an animating force. For many contemporary Continental philosophers, it has become re-recognized as a fecund source.

Regarding Hume's own texts, I shall work primarily with the two *Enquiries* and with the essay "Of the Standard of Taste."[20] As will soon become clear, I do not enter the various debates within Hume scholarship, many or most of which involve the *Treatise*. The scholarship enters where it serves to clarify matters that are addressed in the account. *David Hume: Platonic Philosopher, Continental Ancestor* is almost exclusively a work of interpretation—or more precisely—reinterpretation along lines that have not been explored previously. In no way should these remarks be taken to imply the slightest disrespect to the superb and scrupulous work of Hume scholars. I just happen to see his work very differently.

My first main chapter, examining the *Enquiry Concerning Human Understanding*,[21] seeks to explore the nature of the philosopher in a general way, and to read Hume in what I call a rigorously Humean fashion. I shall argue, for example, that the emergence of natural instinct in the midst of the inquiry is a *deus ex machina,* and that the sudden irruption of final causality into the reflections of the Pyrrhonian skeptic is altogether outside the limits to which Hume prescribed for the human understanding. When one jettisons both, a Hume who is both self-consistent and more interesting emerges: a radical philosopher of imagination.

The same result obtains from my second main chapter, on the *Enquiry Concerning the Principles of Morals.*[22] Here the outcome is more obvious, as it follows directly from Hume's opening page and recurs throughout the several sections. Unlike the first *Enquiry,* in which the preeminent role of images becomes clear only after a style of exegesis in which the text is read against itself, Hume's second *Enquiry* approximates a system, in which the individual virtues are drawn from a dyad in the human heart, that is, *images* of right and wrong, which dwell in every—or almost every—human breast. Hume both proceeds imagistically and employs images in order to engage and to convince. The moral life presents itself as shining image.

Finally, Hume's philosophy of art moves in a somewhat different direction. The question concerns *taste* and not creativity. The search for a standard differs from the *Enquiries* in this important respect, that here the procedure must be regressive. That is, it must move backward from the establishment of the matter of fact that there *is* a standard to those conditions that would satisfy it. These conditions are very demanding indeed, as will be shown. The artworks (primarily literary) that occupy Hume's attention can be called images in a very restricted sense: they are regarded as imitations of sentiments. We have an irony that runs through Hume's thought: the two *Enquiries* display an ultimately aesthetic character, while the aesthetic philosophy moves within a much more traditional rational/empirical circle.

All three chapters abound with recourses to Socratic ignorance. When viewed across the history of philosophy, the emphatic rebirth of this theme holds sway over his responses to other modern philosophers. His fellow major empiricists claimed insights that Hume and Socrates did not. Locke, for example, claimed that if our organs were finer, we could perceive the transition from cause to effect. Berkeley claimed that our notions had a divine source. The major rationalists had even more insight: Descartes into our intelligible essence, Spinoza into the essence of God, Leibniz into preestablished harmony. Rereading these thinkers *through Hume,* it is possible to rediscover other aspects of Socratic ignorance in them after all. In our era, in which scientific and—

especially—technological developments often overwhelm our capacity to take their measure, nothing is needed more than the recognition of the limits to which all human knowledge and human effort is given over. There is no clearer modern source for this than the philosophy of David Hume.

One of the most significant developments in Continental thought is the emergence of a philosophy of imagination in which reason is subordinated to imagination.

Deleuze's Hume . . . and Ours
Madness, Retrieval

Introduction

More than a half-century has passed since the appearance of Gilles Deleuze's *Empiricism and Subjectivity: An Essay on Hume's Theory of Human Nature* (1953), one of the very few works that provide a rich vein for Continental philosophy. Its way of approach to Hume is unique and fruitful. The insights yielded from it are both startling and well grounded. It removes Hume from the standard empiricist-naturalist scope of interpretation. Finally, Deleuze provides the necessary seeding for Hume's reentry as an untapped resource for Continental philosophy.[1] Concentrating on what Deleuze has called "the contradiction between imagination and reflection" as a guide, I will attempt to retrieve elements of Hume in order to introduce this book.

    Here I join the tradition of philosophers who are "scandalized" by various shortcomings of those who fall short of their hopes and expectations: I am scandalized . . . nay, outraged . . . nay, rendered apoplectic by the marginalization of Hume in the living history of Continental thought. After all, it was no British empiricist but *Kant* who first saw and most acutely felt the power of Humean thought. His appreciation of its radicalism led him to extend its epistemological challenge to the concept of cause to the entirety of metaphysics, both general and special. Moses Mendelssohn reputedly referred to Kant as "the all-destroyer," although the Ideas of reason—freedom, God, and immortality—are relocated in the realm that has "primacy," the practical realm. With that in mind, one quakes at the epithet Mendelssohn might have ascribed to the unapologetically cheerful Scottish skeptic and (at least in the Judeo-Christian sense)[2] atheist.

    I contend that contrary to appearances, matters stand otherwise with the undoubtedly great minds of German Idealism. Neither Fichte, nor Hölderlin, nor Schelling, nor Hegel had much to say about Hume (although the latter included him as a moment in philosophy's self-unfolding). We cannot, of course, say with any certainty why this is so; our only recourse is to a kind of punditry, that is, it might be the result of a feeling of German philosophical exceptionalism, and/or of the irresistibly seductive openings provided by Kant's thought, and/or of a certain carelessness to which we are all given over, and/or of a certain carefreeness that gave wing to their thought. This much, however, is undeniable: without Hume, there would have been no critical philosophy of Kant. Thus, Hume's thought is the subsoil of German Idealism—if not more.

Hence, the virtual concession of Hume's thought to Anglo-American philosophy is not only unnecessary, but has deprived philosophy of a valuable and striking now-subterranean source. Deleuze has provided great service in unearthing it.

I. Deleuze: Hume in Motion

Hume famously asserts that reason is passive. In Deleuze's account of Hume, this means that reason becomes a feeling—one might say, another feeling belonging to the stream of impressions and ideas. The mind functions as the site of reflection, through which impressions are rendered both less vivid and suitable for their association into the three groupings of resemblance, contiguity, and causality. The key faculty for Deleuze is a fecund imagination that, I will later suggest, drives the Humean text beyond itself from within it.

> We can now see the special ground of empiricism: nothing in the mind transcends human nature, because it is human nature that, in its principles, transcends the mind; nothing is ever transcendental. Association, far from being a product, is a rule of the imagination and a manifestation of its free exercise. It guides the imagination, gives it uniformity, and also constrains it. In this sense, ideas are connected *in* the mind, not *by* the mind.[3]

Note how this differs from even the best doctrinal accounts of Hume. *The Cambridge Companion to Hume* offers a thoughtful appraisal of Hume in which the collected essays are unified by the vision of its astute editor, David Fate Norton. According to Norton, Hume is "the first post-sceptical philosopher of the early modern period,"[4] who sought and located a path between extreme skepticism and overconfident rationalism. References to the role of imagination occur in this worthy volume, as do the suitable modesty of epistemological claims in general. By contrast, Deleuze encounters a dynamic text, in which internal clashes are intrinsic to its subject matter. This is why the modifier "special ground" belongs to his characterization of Hume's empiricism.

Human nature is thought problematically. It is comprised of all sorts of tensions: between things and relations, between imagination and reason, between passions and ideas, between speculation and practice. The "special ground" is a ground that is always shifting. In this light, I credit Deleuze with discovering what I will call *kinetic* empiricism in Hume. His interpretation in *Empiricism and Subjectivity: An Essay on Hume's Theory of Human Nature* seems to move inexorably toward practice rather than theory; his penultimate sentence reads: "Philosophy must constitute itself as the theory of what we are doing, not as a theory of what there is."[5] Nevertheless, his observations within the realm of theory stand on their own.

In *An Enquiry Concerning Human Understanding,* Hume writes:

> Nothing is more free than the imagination of man; and though it cannot exceed that original stock of ideas furnished by the internal and external senses, it has unlimited power of mixing, compounding, separating, and dividing these ideas, in all the varieties of fiction and vision. (*EHU,* 47)

Like no other interpreter to my knowledge, Deleuze ascribes the origin of the threefold principle of the association of ideas—as seen above—to the *free exercise of imagination* itself. This is an example of a philosophical observation that has remained hidden in plain sight: reason is passive; so, too is sensation. If only by default (and not only by default!) imagination is solely endowed with the *power* to act, which here means to mix ideas, to compound, separate, and divide them. Imagination, which exceeds the mind (reason), belongs to human nature as its vital, internally conflicted special ground.

To imagination's unlimited power, Hume ascribes two results: *fictions* and *visions*. Since Deleuze concentrates so heavily on fictions, as I will soon show, how are visions to be distinguished from them? This distinction is hardly easy to discern. The word is little or no help, as *any* sense of "vision" can be interpreted as overlapping with "fiction," especially in Hume's philosophy. There can only be a sliding difference between them, in accord with the way belief is differentiated from fiction only by virtue of the customary conjunction between two objects. Thus, if at any given time we experience once again the conjunction between fire and heat, we *believe* their connection; while at the same given time, if we experience a conjunction between that same fire and the Schubert *Lied* or the Redd Foxx standup routine to which we are listening, the conjunction is fictional, that is to say, there is no such connection and thus no such belief.

II. Deleuze's Hume and Madness

The trope of madness occurs in the crucial Section IV of the first *Enquiry* titled "Sceptical Doubts Concerning the Operations of the Understanding":

> And though none but a fool or madman will ever pretend to dispute the authority of experience, or to reject that great guide of human life, it may surely be allowed a philosopher to have so much curiosity at least as to examine the principle of human nature, which gives this mighty authority to experience . . . (*EHU*, 36)

This particular "philosophical examination" exposes the rational groundlessness—in other words, the irrationality—of the "principle of human nature" in question, namely the principle of causality. As is too well known to require rehearsing the argument, this "principle" is no more and no less than the customary transition in the imagination from one object to its usual attendant, a transition that is felt in the mind. It is an instinct, and not a valid inference.

Can an assured inference be drawn from this result? Indeed it can: the curious philosopher finds herself located in the region of madness and/or folly, or rather on the nether side of both. Philosophy proves here to be an entry into madness, rather than a respite from it. Hume's famous recourse to practical life is no philosophical response strictly speaking, but rather—at least in the first *Enquiry*—an escape from philosophy.

Thus, madness *is* human nature *simpliciter*. Deleuze grasps this outcome with astonishing recognition. He speaks of the "aesthetic game of the imagination and reason,"[6] which is a game that can yield no winner. Imagination and reason contradict one another; no reconciliation is possible. Hume calls the philosophical system "the monstrous offspring of two principles . . . which are both at once embrac'd by the mind, and which are unable mutually to destroy each another" (*THN*, 215). Deleuze writes:

> From the point of view of philosophy, the mind is no longer anything but delirium and madness. There is no complete system, synthesis, or cosmology that is not imaginary. With the belief in the existence of bodies, fiction itself as a principle is opposed to the principles of association: the latter are *principally* instead of be-

ing *subsequently* excessive, as is the case with general rules. Fantasy triumphs. . . . Here, the most insane is still natural. The system is a mad delirium.[7]

That is to say, the relations of resemblance, contiguity, and causality are epistemologically parasitical upon the belief in the existence of bodies—a reading that exposes one of those revelatory textual moments for Continental philosophy in which a text works against itself *productively*. Beginning from the three principles of association, one discovers that the belief in bodies is a fiction; however, the association of ideas presupposes belief in the external existence of bodies insofar as the latter must be regarded as the source of impressions. The argument—if it may properly be called an argument—is not circular: without an anterior belief in bodies, Hume's monstrous empiricism cannot so much as begin.

III. The Situation of Madness

Madness plays a major role in the Platonic dialogues, especially the *Phaedrus* and the *Ion*. In the former, divine madness is the source of the greatest blessings: prophecy, healing from plagues and woes arising from blood guilt, possession by the Muses, and greatest of all *erōs*. The third kind of madness seizes the great poets, as described in the *Ion*, who are quite ordinary when sane and sober. *Erōs* seizes the philosopher. One is tempted to call it philosophy's necessary condition; however, the barest thought of "condition," whether sufficient, necessary, or logical, presupposes *erōs* to some degree. Unlike human madness, which results in lawlessness and harm, divine madness introduces or reintroduces measure (244a–245b).

Modern philosophy, for better and/or for worse, operates virtually if not actually apart from the mythical framework in which Plato and the Presocratics worked. One finds, therefore, nothing corresponding to the division within madness cited above. The chief residue of Greek philosophy animating its modern counterpart is *wonder*, regarded as the origin of philosophy in both Plato and Aristotle, and in the latter as finding its proper completion in knowledge (*epistēmē*). In *Empiricism and Subjectivity: An Essay on Hume's Theory of Human Nature*, Deleuze both excavates and—as if in a *vernissage*—exhibits the most arresting inscription of madness in the modern period.

Can this inscription be superimposed or—perhaps even, as in a palimpsest—discerned beneath its Platonic ancestor? It is difficult to say. Humean madness as disclosed by Deleuze is certainly intrinsic to the philosophical enterprise, but seems to bear little resemblance to *erōs,* although the "curiosity" of which Hume speaks corresponds closely to the wonder spoken of in the *Theaetetus,* the outcome of which is also Socratic:

> The most perfect philosophy of the natural kind only staves off our ignorance a little longer: as perhaps the most perfect philosophy of the moral or metaphysical kind serves only to discover larger portions of it. Thus the observation of human blindness and weakness is the result of all philosophy, and meets us at every turn, in spite of our endeavours to elude or avoid it. (*EHU,* 31)

However, in his praise of the "Academic or Sceptical philosophy," which insists on caution in judging and exercising due discipline with respect to the limits of human knowledge, one can locate at least a trace of Platonic *erōs:* "Every passion is mortified [by such philosophy], except the love of truth; and that passion never is, nor can be, carried to too high a degree" (*EHU,* 41). Thus, if passion is read as *erōs, erōs* and measure are aligned once more. Nowhere else in modern philosophy is this alignment—strongly suggested by Deleuze's text—so straightforwardly present.

In the last chapters of his book, Deleuze argues in concert with Hume for the ultimately ethical and practical character of the latter's thought. However, he draws out a consequence that is certainly already implicit in Hume, but that Hume himself did not see. Here is how Deleuze untangles the monstrous contradiction that bedevils the philosophical system:

> Madness is human nature related to the mind, just as good sense is the mind related to human nature; each one is the reverse of the other. This is the reason why we must reach the depths of madness and solitude in order to find a passage to good sense. [The domain of general rules and beliefs] is the middle and temperate region, where the contradiction between human nature and the imagination already exists, and always subsists . . . but is regulated by possible corrections and resolved through practice.[8]

Toward the end of Part One of the *Treatise,* Hume playfully gives up the bleak and gloomy result of his theoretical philosophy straightaway for a good dinner, a game of backgammon, and conversation between friends, he joins in the laugh at himself for taking his skepticism so seriously and opts instead for a comment on "the whimsical condition of mankind" (*EHU,* 160) in the first *Enquiry.* However, he never abjures a single one of his theoretical conclusions. He seems to provide no bridge between the "melancholy" radical ignorance to which his thought consigns him and the superficial pleasures that so quickly relieve this despondency.

Deleuze locates such a bridge but ultimately eschews it in favor of ethics and practice. It is the bridge of madness. The delirium of the philosophical system is precisely what gives impetus to "good sense," that is, to its temperance, by means of certain general ideas of the mind. If these moderating ideas are absent, then madness occurs in a region where it can become harmful. However, there neither is nor should there be a "remedy" for madness. Such a cure, happily impossible in principle, would end human nature once and for all.

Could it be that Hume is as valuable a living ancestor for Continental philosophy as is Kant, who confined his comments on madness to his *Anthropology* but not to his critical philosophy? Is Hume, as well as being a thinker who prepared the way for the greatest advance in the modern era, also a thinker who comes toward us from the future? Deleuze's early book firmly indicates an affirmative answer to both. Its insistence on a rigorous empiricism that admits nothing transcendental, together with its insistence that all duality emerges from within the flow of impressions and ideas—what we today might call phenomenology—yields a madness that inhabits all of our efforts to question, as it undermines the conventional wisdom that regards Hume as primarily a naturalist. If, as Hume says, nature is stronger than any principle, that is because of the madness residing at the heart of human nature.

How may we think this madness in our contemporary context? In his own context, madness is presented as the outcome of a philosophical system that would unite reason and imagination but cannot. Reversing yet preserving Hume, we may think of philosophical system-building itself as a manifestation of madness, that is, as a creative act so that—in its highest form—a philosophical system can be approached and interpreted as a work of art. Finally, we must not forget the most salient development in this retrieval: that in philosophizing, we find ourselves ecstatically afflicted—like Hume—with folly and madness.

Chapter I

Aspects of
An Enquiry Concerning Human Understanding

A. On Section I: Of the Different Species of Philosophy

The first matter of consequence concerns its designation. It is not "Introduction." It is not "Foreword." It is not "Preface." That is to say, at the very least, that "Section I: Of the Different Species of Philosophy" belongs intrinsically to the Humean text. Though it does not offer the stipulations and the discourses that constitute what are often construed as his doctrines, it serves as the underpinning to the reading of all that will follow. And it is a most unusual guide. It names no predecessor or contemporary. It examines no doctrine. Upon a first and careless reading, one might suppose it to be a sort of light and agreeable appetizer for the entrée to follow. Nothing could be farther than this from the truth.

If one were to take Hume's comments on the status of the easy and the abstruse philosophy straightforwardly, or his praise of the abstruse philosophy in spite of its general disrepute, one would remain utterly perplexed. Hume writes in one place: "This also must be confessed, that the most durable, as well as justest fame, has been acquired by the easy philosophy" (*EHU*, 7). To declare that the easy philosophy, which consists of commonsense maxims, outlasts the renown of those thinkers who attempt to discover the principles that underlie the various realms of human activity, is to state what is obvious. Although the "easy philosophy" has taken many different forms throughout history, its *locus classicus* can be seen as residing in the magniloquent advice of Polonius to Laertes in Shakespeare's *Hamlet*, which I here excerpt:

> Give thy thoughts no tongue,
> Nor any unproportion'd thought his act.
> Be thou familiar, but by no means vulgar . . .
> Give every man thy ear, but few thy voice;
> Take each man's censure, but reserve thy judgment.
> Costly thy habit as thy purse can buy,
> But not express'd in fancy; rich, not gaudy;
> For the apparel oft proclaims the man, . . .
> Neither a borrower, nor a lender be;
> For loan oft loses both itself and friend,
> And borrowing dulls the edge of husbandry.
> This above all: to thine own self be true,
> And it must follow, as the night the day,
> Thou canst not then be false to any man.
> Farewell; my blessing season this in thee! (Act I, Scene iii)

Can it be that Hume claims the *most just* fame for such drivel, or rather, for a "philosophy" suitable to a newspaper advice column or, at best, to a parent-adolescent heart-to-heart talk about "the ways of the world"? Is justice, for Hume, synonymous with pragmatic suggestions on how best to navigate the social shoals?

The "mere" philosopher, by contrast, "is commonly but little acceptable in the world, as being supposed to contribute nothing either to the advantage or pleasure of society" (*EHU*, 8). He stays far from other human beings and considers matters beyond their comprehension. If it were not for the more despised ignoramus, the mere philosopher would be the object of the greatest contempt among mortals. The "most perfect character" is a means between hapless ignorance and useless erudition. Such an ideal character is at home equally in "books, company, and business" (*EHU*, 8). He knows how to converse in a pleasing and inoffensive manner, as his business prospers.

The observation that follows, however, complicates the matter considerably. On one hand, he declares that nature seems to have prohibited researches that require "abstruse thought and profound researches" (*EHU*, 9). This prohibition derives from the narrow limits of human understanding. On the other, he contends the human being is rational and "receives from science his proper food and nourishment" (*EHU*, 8). Thus, if a philosopher seeks principles that might transcend these narrow limits, nature punishes him with "pensive melancholy." This result echoes the Conclusion to Book I of the *Treatise of Human Nature* where, after announcing the results of his study of the understanding, he is left clinging tremulously to a "barren rock, on which I am at present, rather than venture myself upon that boundless ocean, which runs out into immensity" (*THN*, 264). However, the same nature that seems to proscribe abstruse philosophical researches can provide an escape from skeptical gloom, namely, that same social life that Hume held up to mockery.

However, in the *Enquiry* as well as in the *Treatise*, Hume has a great deal to say in favor of the abstruse philosophy. This is hardly surprising insofar as he is among its ablest practitioners in human history.[1] He lists three advantages it bestows. The first is its "subserviency to the easy and humane" (*EHU*, 9), in that it inspires greater exactness in the latter, much as the study of anatomy serves the painter in her representations of the human form despite what he calls the most "hideous and disagreeable objects" (*EHU*, 10). The second is the "spirit of accuracy" (*EHU*, 10) that, if carefully cultivated, suffuses itself throughout all arts and callings in society.[2] These two are surely worth noting, but they require little comment. The third, however, is another matter:

> Were there no advantage to be reaped from these studies beyond the gratification of an innocent curiosity, yet ought not even this to be despised as being an accession to those few safe and harmless pleasures which are bestowed on the human race. The sweetest and most inoffensive path of life leads through the avenues of science and learning.

Then, after briefly noting that most people are not fitted for such obscure study, he adds:

> Obscurity, indeed, is painful to the mind as well as to the eye; but to bring light from obscurity, by whatever labor, must needs be delightful and rejoicing. (*EHU*, 11)

This passage requires the most careful scrutiny. Consider Socrates and the Athenian judges, his fellow citizens who convicted him and sentenced him to death, in one of history's great democracies. In another way, consider the punishment of Copernicus and the burning to death of Bruno during the Middle Ages, which no doubt featured many less famous but equally venal treatments of people engaged in the "few and harmless pleasures" of pursuing wisdom. One cannot even read Descartes without becoming conscious of the delicate balance he attempts to achieve between his philosophical views and the religious authorities of his time. What about Hume? He was said to have many, many friends but few enemies. However, on account of these enemies those friends persuaded him not to permit the publication of his *Dialogues on Natural Religion* until after his death. One can therefore conclude that the desire to satisfy an "innocent curiosity" in philosophy and science is often regarded as far from irreproachable in some quarters.

What Hume calls "the justest and most plausible objection against a considerable part of metaphysics" (*EHU,* 11) involves its not being a real science but rather either an inflated and fruitless exercise into inaccessible regions or a source drawn from within superstition in order to introduce confusion rather than belief. However, he goes on to defend philosophy against these would-be detractors as seeking to "cultivate true metaphysics with some care, in order to destroy the false and adulterated" (*EHU,* 12). His first *Enquiry* is in service to this cultivation, and his famous "mental geography" is its means. It will establish those "narrow limits" within which the human understanding can properly operate, and will consign to oblivion all traces of the "false metaphysics" to which so many philosophers as well as ordinary people have subscribed. Recalling the conclusion to Book I of the *Treatise,* the "abstruse" result proves desultory indeed.

At this point, I return to the "delight and rejoicing" with which Hume associates those investigations that succeed in bringing light from obscurity. The light Hume brings illuminates the human understanding, its nature and its limits. Said in another way, Hume provides another major accomplishment on the path indicated by the Delphic oracle: *gnōthi seauton,* "know yourself." Further, his philosophical studies are innocent and harmless in the genuine sense: they are motivated by nothing other than *philo-sophia,* the love of wisdom and learning. In this way, they recall Socratic philosophy and Socratic practice. In Plato's *Apology of Socrates,* the philosopher (1) declares his knowledge of "important" (i.e., transcendent) matters to = 0 and his wisdom to be "worth little or nothing" (23b), yet (2) tells those who voted for his acquittal that it is their duty to be cheerful *(euelpidas)* (41c)!

Finally and in light of the above, I therefore think that the only sense with which one can read about Hume's despair concerning his lonely residence on a rock in the midst of a limitless ocean is a *playful* sense. But Hume's playfulness, like Plato's, conceals within itself the highest seriousness, and belongs to his philosophy as much as his insights and inferences. Viewed in a preliminary way, the light shed by Hume's thought is not a light that shines brightly on truth, but a light that reveals the *darkness* to which the human understanding has been given over. The pleasure one derives from such a light is of a different order than the pleasures enjoyed by those who share the superlative "most perfect of characters." It might be tentatively characterized as delight and joy taken in the most hard-won human self-knowledge.

Hume's own imperturbable good humor has received much testimony. Most notable is that of his friend Adam Smith, who was with Hume as the latter was awaiting his impending death:

> His cheerfulness was so great, and his conversation and amusements run so much in their usual strain, that, notwithstanding all bad symptoms, many people could not believe he was dying. "I shall tell your friend, Colonel Edmondstone," said Doctor Dundas to him one day, "that I left you much better, and in a fair way of recovery." "Doctor," said he, "as I believe you would not choose to tell any thing but the truth, you had better tell him, that I am dying as fast as my enemies, if I have any, could wish, and as easily and cheerfully as my best friends could desire."

Smith concludes his letter with words that echo those rehearsed by Phaedo at the end of that eponymous dialogue:

> Upon the whole, I have always considered him, both in his lifetime and since his death, as approaching as nearly to the idea of a perfectly wise and virtuous man, as perhaps the nature of human frailty will permit.[3]

I continue my consideration of Hume's Section I by examining his imaginary exhortation from nature: "Be a philosopher; but, amidst all your philosophy, be still a man" (*EHU,* 9). Recall that this exhortation follows nature's proscription regarding the abstruse philosophy, which it will punish with despondency. Thus, it is contrary to nature to be *both* an abstruse philosopher *and* a man, though no such difficulty obtains for those who practice the easy philosophy. Thus, when read accurately, the exhortation reads: you can be an abstruse philosopher, in which case you cannot be a man; or you can be a man, it which case you cannot be an abstruse philosopher. This reading echoes another aspect of Hume's conclusion to Book I of the *Treatise,* in which he imagines himself to be "some strange uncouth monster, who not being able to mingle and unite in society, has been expell'd all human commerce, and left utterly abandon'd and disconsolate" (*THN,* 264).

This is, of course, hardly the end; to our great relief, Hume did not remain on his rock but returned to society. This is an ambiguously philosophical return. In one of its aspects, it consists of taking part in habitual pleasures, such as a game of backgammon or the conviviality of meeting with friends.

In the other, the abstruse philosopher takes over from the social human being when the being in question repairs to his life apart from such natural pleasures. The abstruse philosopher's concerns cannot help but resurface. The passion for accuracy makes itself felt. So too does the kindred passion for correcting the errors of the learned that impact so many other fields. The sapient philosopher appears to be two, not one—or at least not one with himself.

Hume regarded the first *Enquiry* as providing a mere alternative to the prolixity of the *Treatise*. However, Section I of the first *Enquiry* makes a subtle but significant addition. He writes that based on the success achieved in mapping the heavens that are so distant from us, we can hope for success in the quest for an accurate mental geography. He calls it "probable" that upon very careful inner inspection, one operation or principle will be found to depend on another, etc. In his concluding words to Section I that require close inspection, he makes the aforementioned addition almost in passing:

> Happy, if we can unite the boundaries of the different species of philosophy, by reconciling profound enquiry with clearness, and truth with novelty! And still more happy, if, *reasoning in this easy manner*, we can undermine the foundations of an abstruse philosophy, which seems to have hitherto served only as a shelter to superstition, and a cover to absurdity and error! (*EHU*, 16; emphasis mine)

This, passage provokes several responses:

1. The reasoning Hume will offer in his first *Enquiry*, he claims, belongs to the *easy* species of philosophy. This will come as news both to students and to generations of Hume scholars who have lived well-spent lives wrestling with the thought contained therein.

2. That Hume's "happiness" is conditional (twice) must be noted. And it is at least arguable whether either condition has been fully met, and to what degree each has been met, and even whether either or both have been met at all. In my reading, Hume meets both demanding conditions. I would rather say the only other philosopher who, with Hume, can lay claim to having provided the most profound philosophical examinations in the clearest language is Plato. There are almost no difficult Greek words in Plato; yet Platonic thought is not only an influential part of our history, but remains and will remain very much alive and part of our contemporary philosophical life. Hume's English, while sounding somewhat dated and, to American ears, a bit unusual, is nevertheless wholly accessible at least in the *Enquiries*.

3. His remark on "an abstruse philosophy, which seems to have hitherto served only as a shelter to superstition, and a cover to absurdity and error"

includes an important disclaimer. First, the word *an* does not refer to the abstruse philosophy to which Hume earlier ascribed three clear virtues. While he does not give a precise reference here, he quite obviously refers to some version of what he earlier called "false metaphysics," whether it is a version of Scholasticism or of some version of an all-denying skepticism that opens the way to blind ignorance.

I will try to assemble the parts in order to determine what—or who—a philosopher is for Hume. After this assembly is completed, we shall discover that "philosopher" does not primarily refer to a particular person or to a specific practice. Rather, it points to a certain image within which two quite different elements combine. In the end, as I will attempt to show, an uncanny unity secures this image.

As practicing the abstruse philosophy apart from society, a philosopher is monstrous, distant from and unsuitable for the humanity into which he was born. However, as also practicing the easy philosophy—which he does simply by acting in accord with such common beliefs as the reality of sensible things and the causal principle—he is indeed a human being. Finally, he strives to split the difference. The first *Enquiry* seeks "happiness" in uniting profundity with clarity and truth with novelty. The means of its pursuit is, once again, "reasoning in this easy manner." The result, in terms of "profundity" and "truth," is the most complete undermining not only of bad abstruse philosophy but of all common belief. In a word, it is madness.

The investigation of the vaunted "principle of causality" results in its reduction to an entirely subjective process involving constant conjunction and belief. Regarding the objects of sensation, we cannot know whether they are given as they really are, we cannot know whether they resemble some originals, and we have no grounds at all to choose between these alternatives. In the conclusion to Book I of the *Treatise*, Hume wrote: "Philosophy . . . if just, can present us only with mild and moderate sentiments" (*THN,* 272). Its analogue, the first *Enquiry*, ends with a call to consign a great many books to the flames.

I conclude consideration of Section I by attending to Hume's notion of *happiness* with the preceding in mind. Its only echo in philosophy's history is the Platonic one, in the figure of Socrates. In the *Apology*, Socrates makes the extraordinary claim that on the one hand the Olympic victors only make his fellow citizens *seem* to be happy *(eudaimonas dokein einai),* while on the other hand "I make you *be* happy *(egō de einai)*" (36d). In this sense, happiness could hardly be farther from the sense of ease belonging to the person Hume mocked earlier in this section, the man who was at home equally in "books, company, and business." Rather, happiness is *eu-daimonia*: spiritually well, standing in good spiritual stead. Genuine human happiness requires "[a]ccurate and just reasoning [which] is the only catholic remedy, fitted for all persons and all dispositions" (*EHU,* 12). This accurate and just reasoning *includes* the twists in his prose, the sharp ironies, the subtle ridicule of his fellow citizens. They are worthy of the Socrates who provokes madness of the human kind in Alcibiades as the latter describes him in the *Symposium.* As introducing measure, that is, by insisting on the moderation that properly follows his still stupefying insights and outrageous prose, he recalls the Socrates of the *Phaedrus* who praises the four kinds of divine madness for their introduction of measure into what was previously turmoil and wreckage.

Since "all persons and all dispositions" are capable of undertaking the inquiry, there is no exit from the obligation to philosophize, that is, to subject one's thoughts to the most thorough examination. Shirking that obligation involves shirking one's essential humanity. And nature, according to Hume, has been gracious enough to provide a measure for this examination: if the outcome produces pain—melancholy—the way of its undertaking has been mistaken. As Socrates said toward the end of the *Apology:* "It is necessary to be cheerful, judges, when facing death, and to think this one truth, that no evil can happen to a good man, either in life or after death" (41c–d). In a very different context but in the same spirit, we behold Hume's famous affirmation of his life and good cheer on his deathbed.

B. Aspects of Section II: Of the Origin of Ideas

Hume *stipulates* his vocabulary. Its words have both denotative and connotative definitions. He accepts the "common" denomination of the words "thought or ideas." The word for their origin requires further explanation, as there is no word for it in English or, he says, in most other languages:

> Let us, therefore, use a little freedom, and call them *Impressions*; employing that word in a sense somewhat different from the usual. By the term *impression,* then, I mean all our more lively perceptions, when we hear, or see, or feel, or love, or hate, or desire, or will. And impressions are distinguished from ideas, which are the less lively perceptions, of which we are conscious, when we reflect on any of those sensations or movements above mentioned. (*EHU,* 18)

Two matters stand in exquisite tension as they arise clearly from this text. (1) The difference between impressions and ideas is a difference in degree only, that is, a difference on a scale of liveliness or force. One might well regard it as a quantitative difference, though it seems that there must be some point of equilibrium at which it is impossible to distinguish an impression from an idea. (2) Although liveliness and force seem to be the criteria by which impressions and ideas are distinguished, Hume also introduces a qualitative distinction: impressions have their source in the human capacity to sense, to feel, and to will directly. Ideas or thoughts are conscious as they arise from *reflection* on those "sensations or movements." This does not represent any confusion on Hume's part. Rather, it is another display of his irreproachable scrupulousness in detailing the paradoxical framework within which he will philosophize. Recalling Section I, it is *easy* to follow Hume's discourse, however difficult the matters he considers.

Given this framework, it is not especially taxing to find ways to criticize this division, and many have done so. However, this activity can only bear witness to a misunderstanding of Hume, and a more general misunderstanding of how to try to think along with great thinkers. The latter task requires entering into the thinker's discourse in its own terms, so far as this is possible. This means that Hume's stipulations must be *accepted as presented*. Such acceptance requires little effort. After all, basic logic courses everywhere teach their students that stipulative definitions have no truth value. Why grant Hume's stipulations? Several reasons present themselves. First, we can locate the distinction between impressions and ideas *in ourselves* without recourse to argument and thus without difficulty. Secondly, this distinction is never presented as *true* as opposed to false. Rather, it provides the framework within which matters of truth and falsity can occur.

Finally and most crucially, this distinction reduces the degree of assumption to its absolute minimum. The only concession to Hume's discourse involves admitting that among one's conceptions some are livelier than others, and that the more lively ones come from sensation. I regard this minimal positing as a *purification* rather than a correction of what is called British empiricism. It delimits the notion of *idea* to the less lively perceptions, thereby cleansing it of its more promiscuous sense in Locke, and of a Berkeleyan "Author of Nature" who enables the distinction between genuine and false perceptions. More provocatively, it also calls into question but does not entirely discard Locke's sharp separation between the ideas of sensation and the ideas of reflection. Impressions and ideas are in one sense homogeneous, differing only in degree, and in another but perhaps at the same time heterogeneous, differing in kind. In terms of the human condition, this is the most we can assert with any confidence.

Hume does not speak of the human condition, but rather of *human nature*. This latter designation, as we will see before too long, is interpretively laden to such an enormous degree and to such a sedimented degree that it is almost excusable to remain blind to it. Hume's "theory" of philosophy is almost universally regarded as "naturalism," the way "capitalism" or "socialism" are regarded as theories of economics. There is so very much in Hume that works against any such characterization that it is either false or misleading. Search as you will, and you will find no significant parallels in Hume either to the natural sciences that he playfully purports to imitate, or to the mathematical sciences of his time, or to the moral philosophy of his time. His aesthetics is a somewhat different case, but it, too, issues in Socratic ignorance. Rather, each of these studies, including the first *Enquiry* in an exemplary fashion, issues in the result that human wisdom is worth little or nothing, and that this result is an occasion for cheerfulness.

There may seem to be a large gulf between the apparent affirmation of what is normally translated as formal cause in Plato, and its dismissal in favor of efficient cause in Hume. The gulf is not large at all, however, as I will now attempt to demonstrate. This is hardly surprising, given the like magnitude of their thought. In the *Phaedo,* Socrates recounts his youthful infatuation with natural science, an infatuation that left him utterly confused. Seizing with great hope upon the account of intellect *(Nous),* which Anaxagoras proposed as the cause of all things, further disappointment ensued. Anaxagoras mistook the condition for the cause. Out of this thoroughgoing aporia, Socrates developed a method of his own. I highlight the key words:

> This was the *method* which I adopted: I first assumed some principle (*logon*) which I judged to be the strongest (*errōmenestaton),* and then *I affirmed as true* whatever *seemed to agree* with this, whether relating to the cause or to anything else; and that which disagreed I regarded as untrue. But I should like to explain my meaning clearly, as I do not think that you understand me.
>
> No, indeed, replied Cebes, not very well.
>
> There is nothing new, he said, in what I am about to tell you; but only what I have been always and everywhere repeating in the previous discussion and on other thoughts, and I shall have to go back to those familiar words which are in the mouth of everyone, and *first of all assume* that there is an absolute beauty and goodness and greatness, and the like; *grant me this,* and I hope to be able to show you the nature of the cause, and to prove the immortality of the soul. (100a–e; emphasis mine)

What is a *method? Methodos* in Greek denotes a way or path. *Hodos* means "road." It is an "easy" word. But the "bigger," "easier" word is "I." Socrates thereby inscribes his path into the pursuit of wisdom, where it yet remains. Why does it yet remain? Because of its strength, its health. *Errōmenestaton* means strongest, healthiest. It is strongest both because it is presupposed in all contests of *logoi, erga,* and *aisthēta* and because it is victorious in any contest of *logoi* where it is disputed. Note that there is no claim whatsoever concerning its ultimate truth. The contrary, rather, is implicitly asserted in the various "I . . ." and "me" passages. These are the Socratic minima, which, like their Humean counterparts, are asserted, that is, stipulated.

To what, then, does the method lead? It leads only to *some* relief from the confusion in which Socrates found himself in his investigations of causes. The full measure of the limits of this method are captured in Socrates' own characterization of it in other places: *eikē phurō*, "random mixing" (97b). There arises what can only be called a small measure of clarity regarding causes within the overriding confusion. What causes a tall woman to be tall? Her participation in the *eidos* tallness. What causes her to be a woman? Her participation in womanness. I hasten to add that the word translated as "cause" here has much broader significance in ancient Greek though than it does for us. The primary sense of *aitia* given in *LSJ* is "charge" or "accusation," as in the case of a crime committed; in other words, its sense is one of "attribution." The second meaning listed is the "philosophical" one, cause (Plato is cited). Third is "an occasion," or "opportunity." To ascribe what is thought in *aitia* as cause in our sense alone is to overinterpret and to narrow what the Greeks heard in it.[4]

Is Hume correct in dismissing formal causes as causes? Yes, if the notion of causality is restricted to *efficient* causality alone. No, if the sedimented interpretive content is excavated and set aside. There is a twisted journey from the Greek notion of *aitia* to "efficient cause." Accurate translations of the four Greek *aitiai* as they occur in Aristotle's *Physics* would be close to the following: that from which (*to ex ou gignetai*)—*hulē*; that into which—the *eidos* and the *paradeigma;* that which initiates change or rest—*hē archē tēs metabolēs hē prōtē ē tēs ēremēseōs;* the end or purpose, that for the sake of which something is done—*to telos . . . to ou heneka.*[5] These were rendered, through their latinization, as "material cause," "formal cause," "efficient cause," and "final cause." It seems to me to be one of the most profound ironies in the history of philosophy that Hume, whose contempt for Scholastic metaphysics could hardly be exceeded, employed a rusticated concept of causality bequeathed by the very philosophical tradition he loathed. However, great thinker that he is, he did not really employ it. Rather, he took it up in such a way as to *render it entirely unintelligible.* The outcome: upon inspection, both the Socratic and the Humean causes disappear. Hume's recourse to nature and to natural instinct is an admission of utter philosophical defeat. In other words, the philosophical outcome is close in deed to the Platonic outcome: a wondrous reaffirmation of Socratic ignorance.⁶

I turn briefly to Section II and its conclusion. Impressions, as strong and vivid, are much more easily discerned than ideas, which are fainter and more obscure by comparison. Hume presents a criterion for determining whether a philosophical term has meaning or not:

> When we entertain . . . any suspicion that a philosophical term is employed without any meaning or idea (as is but too frequent), we need but enquire, *from what impression is that supposed idea derived?* And if it be impossible to assign any, this will serve to confirm our suspicion. By bringing ideas into so clear a light we may reasonably hope to remove all dispute, which may arise, concerning their nature and reality. (*EHU*, 22)

This test, so simple yet so rich with matters of the greatest consequence (even for Hume!), establishes precisely the role to be played by the original framework of Hume's philosophical inquiries. If one is fortunate enough to be able to return to this text as if reading it for the first time, free of the blinders and misunderstandings handed down by the dominant tradition of scholarship, one will receive unprecedented delight as well as bountiful insight.

C. Aspects of Section III: Of the Association of Ideas

Appearance in "memory or imagination" associates ideas. In a thought-provoking observation, Hume declares: "[E]ven in our wildest and most wandering reveries, nay in our very dreams, we shall find, if we reflect, that the imagination ran not altogether at adventures" (*EHU*, 23). That is, there occurs always *some* clumping of ideas. This seemingly modest proclamation seems both clear and innocuous, but will prove to have major—if not alarming—ramifications. Resemblance: Hume gives the example of the way a picture is associated with its original. Contiguity: mention of one apartment leads to conversation about those next to it. Cause and effect: thinking of a wound brings about thought of the attendant pain.

However, one again finds some ambiguity in the stipulated divisions of association. Resemblance could well include cause and effect in Hume's example. Contiguity could well be included in Hume's example of causality. And in any case, there is nothing in the notion of association of ideas that excludes what was earlier called an "adventure" of the imagination. A picture may just as easily resemble another picture of an entirely different subject, which then leads to consideration of a contiguous event, from which follows a causal account. My example: a picture of Van Gogh's sunflowers leads instantaneously to fields of sunflowers in central Italy which, in turn, leads to thoughts of corruption caused by organized crime.

In this early section, the most important of the three principles, cause and effect, has not yet been subject to critique. However, in the added sections to editions K, L, and N, we are provided with important glimpses into "a field of speculation more entertaining, and perhaps more instructive, than the other,"[7] that is, more than the earlier threefold delineation that Hume considered complete. This addition treats what Hume calls the unity imposed by imagination. Genius is insufficient for the production of artworks,[8] all of which must display a connection between the parts that renders the work whole and one, as well as worthy of the consideration of humankind. Among the three principles of association, causality has priority at this point.

Whether one writes a history of any period, a biography (even of a fictional character such as Achilles), or a poem, the events must be presented with sufficient causal intelligibility to engage the reader. After a fascinating discourse on the construction of epic poetry that involves the poet's inflaming the passions of readers while presenting the various causal connections within proper measure, Hume draws a "more entertaining, and perhaps more instructive" inference concerning the difference between history and epic poetry:

> As the difference, therefore, betwixt history and epic poetry consists only in the degrees of connection which bind together those several events of which their subject is composed, it will be difficult, if not impossible, *by words* to determine exactly the bounds which separate them from each other. That is a matter of taste more than of reasoning; and perhaps this unity may often be discovered in a subject where, at first view, and from an abstract consideration, we should least expect to find it.[9]

Hume's examples are Homer's *Iliad* and Milton's *Paradise Lost*, two works that hold an important place in his essay on aesthetic taste, which will be examined in the third chapter. Both works find the poet traveling far from the initial impetus driving the poems, the rage of Achilles in the former and the creation of the world in the latter. Nevertheless, the distance traveled from these beginnings serves to heighten rather than diminish interest in the unfolding of the narrative. Though he does not expressly say this, the unity of the great poems is sustained without the temporal unity of causes that one finds in the great histories. However, Hume never claims that the distinction between poetry and history belongs to the nature of the different kinds of writing but only to the degree to which unity occurs in each—unity that is discernable by taste alone, for the movement of the passions determines which is which—for they are not determinable in principle, or "in words."

I say: the unity is entirely a unity of imagery. This becomes clear in the upcoming discussion on *belief*.

D. Aspects of Section IV: Sceptical Doubts Concerning the Operations of the Understanding, Section V: Sceptical Solution of These Doubts, and Section VII: Of the Idea of Necessary Connexion

In the brief but decisive first part of this section, Hume aligns his thought with Socratic ignorance, from which it has already taken its departure and within which it will always remain. To remind:

> The most perfect philosophy of the natural kind only staves off our ignorance a little longer: as perhaps the most perfect philosophy of the moral or metaphysical kind serves only to discover larger portions of it. Thus the observation of human blindness and weakness is the result of all philosophy, and meets us at every turn, in spite of our endeavors to elude or avoid it. (*EHU*, 31)

What, precisely, is "philosophy of the natural kind"? On the frontpiece of the *Treatise*, Hume characterizes his thought as "Being An Attempt to Introduce the Experimental Method of Reasoning Into Moral Subjects." Natural philosophy, in the first third of the eighteenth century, referred to what we would today call "natural science," which comprehended Newtonian physics most eminently together with the contributions of the physicist (and mechanist) Boyle and others. The scholarship on the Hume-Newton intellectual relation is spirited and learned. Ironically, it can produce nothing certain regarding the degree to which Hume adopted a Newtonian methodological model, despite Hume's frequently acknowledged and supreme admiration for Newton's genius.

"Moral subjects" referred to *human* matters. Unlike those matters that occupy physics, Hume's "natural philosophy" does not have a single calculation. It neither arrives at a single "principle" or law nor does it make a single prediction, unless it "predicts" the failure of any attempt to transcend what is called the "narrow . . . bounds of human understanding" (*EHU*, 8). There is, therefore, an unavoidable tension in the word *natural* when it is concerned with human things. Hume's thought displays this tension despite—or precisely on account of—its bond to the human understanding. To speak crudely, bodies are objects; their constitution and their behavior can therefore be measured quantitatively to some degree. Hume lists those few "general causes" of bodies in nature that we can hope to know: "Elasticity, gravity, cohesion of parts, communication of motion by impulse; these are probably the ultimate causes and principles which we shall ever discover in nature"(*EHU*, 30). He insists, however, that we cannot ascend beyond causes of this kind (the subsequent developments of physics remain within this scope). Ultimate "springs and principles" are "totally shut up from human curiosity and enquiry" (*EHU*, 30).

The human understanding, to use Hume's word, is something *other*. Unlike certain of his analytic heirs and their brain-loving brethren, Hume has no doubt that there *is* such an understanding, and that its own nature and limits can be delineated. Physics yields knowledge of bodies. Philosophy as such yields self-knowledge. Physical knowledge can expand; self-knowledge generally involves contraction, awareness of one's own ineluctable human limits. Heraclitus: "No matter if you travel down every path of soul, you will never discover all: so deep is its *logos*." *(Psuchēs peirata iōn ouk an exeuroio, pasan epiporeuomenos hodon. Houtō bathun logon echei.)*[10] However, in light of Hume's own thought, the first sentence of this paragraph must be rewritten. As all "natural philosophy" presupposes the operations of the human understanding, bodies—"nature"—understood as distinct from understanding, are *other*. More radically yet, it is not at all clear that "nature" in the latter sense is other at all from the human understanding.

How, then, to understand "nature"? In Hume's thought, it seems as if it is so well understood as to require no explanation. He is certainly no Aristotelian, nor is he a Platonist in the usual sense. To gain access to the sense of "nature" here operative, I strongly suggest that we return to the sedimented but still alive Greek sense of *phusis* as derived from *phuō*, to come to light. Both "nature" as the object of physics and "human nature" *come to light*. And as coming to light, both are shrouded by a certain darkness. In physics, the darkness is inscribed by the inaccessibility of "secret springs and principles." In self-knowledge, the light serves to illuminate the darkness that runs through and through.

Hume's, then, is an *ironic* natural philosophy. Let us grant, as we must if we are to hear him, his distinction among the "objects of Enquiry" between relations of ideas, the opposites of which involve a contradiction, and matters of fact, the opposites of which do not involve a contradiction. Let us also grant that this distinction exhausts the possibilities among these objects. Let us further grant that the relation of cause and effect is the only basis of reasoning concerning matters of fact. That is, without the idea of cause and effect, we would have nothing other than present sensation and memory to guide us. Let us leave aside all future philosophical commentary and criticism, including Kant's Second Analogy of Experience. The outcome—well-known but always surprising, is that no reasoning can account for our experience of matters of fact.

Cause and effect cannot be a relation of ideas, since cause means "necessary connection," and since no matter of fact is such that its attendant cannot be otherwise but is contingent. Nor can the idea of cause and effect be a matter of fact. Any two constantly conjoined events can be said to be connected only on the assumption that the future will resemble the past. And the resemblance of the future to the past is precisely the matter in question concerning the idea of cause and effect. Therefore, as assuming what must be proven, the argument is circular, as Hume observes. The only possible conclusion is the skeptical one: the idea of cause and effect escapes all reasoning and all processes of the understanding.

In one of the passages that are often either misread or expressed unclearly, Hume writes the following of the general propositions that constitute cause and effect:

> These two propositions are *far* from being the same, I have found that such an object has always been attended with such an effect, and I foresee, that other objects, which are, in appearance, similar, will be attended with similar effects. I shall allow, *if you please,* that the one proposition may justly be inferred from the other: I know, in fact, that it always is inferred. (*EHU,* 34; emphasis mine)

He proceeds to claim, however, that this "inference" is neither intuitive, that is, immediate, nor is there a "medium," namely, an intermediate noncircular premise or group of premises. Inference: what does it mean? *In-ferra,* in the Latin, means "bring into," and by the sixteenth century was associated with the notion of cause—but this notion is precisely what Hume here calls into question.

Students in basic logic classes worldwide are misdirected into supposing that there are two species of logical inference and that "induction" is one of them. It should be clear enough that the insertion of a premise asserting the *probable* similarity of future to past suffers from the same fateful defect. Understood properly, there is simply no way to render intelligible the transition from the memory of past events to their similar recurrence in the future.

Hume's "allowance" of the justice of this so-called inference does not change this. Read strictly, he offers a mere conditional. This is one of the very few places where Hume's text *can* mislead, and *has* misled generations of scholars. It is one of the coarsest *non sequiturs* in philosophy's history to conclude that in spite of its argumentation, one can believe that there *really are* causes and effects in nature although we cannot account for this idea.

E. Aspects of Section V: Sceptical Solution of These Doubts

Hume begins by noting that the passion for philosophy carries with it the danger that it can result in an exalted selfishness, that is, in sitting on a perch from which the purported sage looks down upon the pursuits of ordinary mortals and cultivates an indolent superiority, as happened with Epictetus and the Stoics in his opinion. He praises what he calls "the Academic or Sceptical philosophy" for its moderation:

> The academics always talk of doubt and suspense of judgment, of danger in hasty determinations, of confining to very narrow bounds the enquiries of the understanding, and of renouncing all speculations which lie not within the limits of common life and practice. . . . Every passion is mortified by it, except the love of truth; and that passion never is, nor can be, carried to too high a degree. It is surprising, therefore, that this philosophy, which, in almost every instance, must be harmless and innocent, should be the subject of so much groundless reproach and obloquy. (*EHU*, 41)

Once again, what Hume calls the "Academic or Sceptical philosophy" sounds closely akin to Socratic ignorance. Such philosophy explicitly and/or implicitly undermines any claim of special knowledge, including religious knowledge. In so doing, its innocence translates into its vulnerability. Every species of dogma, hearing a call to account for itself and finding itself unable to do so, rebels angrily against it. Recall Thrasymachus's response to Socrates' profession of ignorance and his request for the former's definition of justice:

> How characteristic of Socrates! he replied, with a bitter laugh;— that's your ironical style! Did I not foresee—have I not already told you, that whatever he was asked he would refuse to answer, and try irony or any other shuffle, in order that he might avoid answering? (337a)

Hume claims here that the passion for truth (a) can never be excessive and (b) results in modesty and moderation. In the following, I shall examine two different assumptions serially. In the first, I will grant, with Hume, that we do infer effects from their causes. In the second, I will not grant this, but rather will trace Hume's argumentation as if the notion of causality was not inscribed into philosophy from its beginning to the present but rather *suspended*, in order to see what the outcome would be *using Hume's apparatus alone*. I suggest strongly that this assumption yields a result more in keeping with Hume's passion for truth.

First, we do, *in fact*, infer effects from causes. But how can we do so, if we must conclude that this inference in not based on rational grounds? Nature! "Nature will always maintain her rights, and prevail in the end over any abstract reasoning whatsoever" (*EHU*, 41). But what is Hume claiming? He claims that, however decisively reasoned the arguments are that deny the connection of cause and effect, "there is no danger that these reasonings, on which almost all knowledge depends, will ever be affected by such a discovery" (*EHU*, 41). What then? Custom! And then? Belief! One must admire Hume for the unpretentiousness of his language, which again recalls the ordinariness of Platonic Greek. Like Platonic Greek, however, this language provokes many questions and demands much attention.

And "nature!" But let us ask once again, "What is nature?" this time in terms of Hume's specific nomenclature. Nature is not an impression. In no sense does anything like "nature" present itself vividly to sense experience. Is nature an idea? If it is an idea, it is so vague and so exceptionally differentiated that it is an especially weak idea, and perhaps does not qualify as an idea at all. It is a reflection on impressions of . . . just about everything! This is the only answer we can give to the decisive Humean question: *"From what impression is that supposed idea derived?"* (*EHU*, 22), and it is not satisfactory at all.

Suddenly, nature possesses a peculiar agency. Its status shifts from being a problematic idea to being the source that overrides what appear to be the unavoidable results of Hume's convincing skeptical argumentation. We cannot know? But no worry—we can act! Nor do we require any philosophical justification to act or, for that matter, for the inference from informed ignorance to action is both dictated and enforced by . . . nature!: "Nature will always maintain her rights" (*EHU*, 41) over any abstract reasoning. This statement is asserted without proof, as if it was self-evident to all. What sort of proposition is "Nature will always maintain her rights"? It falls entirely outside the Humean schema of impressions and ideas. However, this and statements like it form the basis of the conventional and virtually unchallenged wisdom that Hume is a "naturalist" of some kind.

But recall: Hume insists that the skeptical or academical method resists quick conclusions and favors step-by-step progress using the plainest propositions. Still more insistently, he isolates the passion for truth as the *only* passion that can never be excessive. In this light, the sudden recourse to a natural impulse that overrides all abstract reasoning is—or should be seen as—another startling non sequitur. What has blinded so many learned people? Their own natural impulses, perhaps? But this is not philosophy; this is not love of truth. This is a *deus ex machina,* employed to fill the empty space disclosed by the limits of our rational faculties. It is one thing to say "The workings of the idea of cause and effect cannot be known" and quite another to say that a "natural impulse" such as "custom" is its analogue, or at least is the origin of our belief in it.

If Hume is or wanted to be a "naturalist," whatever that is, he could have *begun* by asserting natural instinct as the source of all human activity, and relegated his critique of the understanding to the margins, where it would belong. But he did not. What he has given us is a genuine philosophical text, that is, a text that exceeds what it would contain. It is a text like Kant's, Fichte's, or Schelling's—or Berkeley's—that on account of its very rigor and fidelity to its subject matter, *works against itself.*

F. Aspects of Section VII: Of the Idea of Necessary Connexion

This brings us to the second of the two pathways proposed above, assuming that the notion of causality was not inscribed into philosophy from its beginning to the present but rather *suspended* in order to see if an alternative outcome would ensue. Following Hume, we will seek that . . . "something" that enables us to surpass our present sensation and our memory so that they can be rendered useful to us, that is, so that they can serve as guides to the future. From our combined sensation and memory, we find certain events constantly conjoined. Some of the more obvious ones are fire and heat; some of the more obscure ones might include atabrine and malaria; some of the more average ones might be wealth and material comfort. Some of the ones so common that we scarcely if ever think of them are opening a spigot and seeing water flow from it, or seeing snow on the ground and anticipating that the weather outside will be cold.

> But there is nothing in a number of instances, different from every single instance, which is supposed to be exactly similar; except only, that after a repetition of similar instances, the mind is

carried by habit, upon the appearance of one event, to expect its usual attendant, and to believe that it will exist. This connexion, therefore, which we *feel* in the mind, this customary transition of the imagination from one object to its usual attendant, is the sentiment or impression from which we form the idea of power or necessary connexion. Nothing farther is in the case. (*EHU*, 75)

I propose to examine this crucial passage in the genuine Humean skeptical spirit. That is, I propose to let Hume speak in a consistently Humean manner, a manner that dares to question matters that both "the vast generality of mankind" and "the learned" take for granted. First, does the feeling of the connection of the mind, to wit, this transition of imagination, that is, does this "sentiment or impression" beget the idea of cause and effect? First answer: there is certainly no necessary connection between what Hume will soon—and strangely—call this "new" impression and the idea of cause and effect. It is entirely plausible to say that the idea of cause and effect arises from the repeated readings of Western philosophy since Aristotle in which the issue of cause and effect plays a central role. That is, it is altogether plausible to conclude that this "feeling" or "new sentiment" is nothing more than the product of that repeated repetition of which Hume speaks. In that sense, cause and effect is more than merely a weak idea. It is a fiction developed by an unbound imagination, located among ghosts and angels and not distinguishable from beliefs at all.

Further, is the experience of constant conjunction plus habit or custom in the imagination even an impression at all? Given Hume's nomenclature, it is impossible to say. An impression is merely a more lively perception, and "feeling" is included within the scope of perception. And for an idea to have meaning requires that it be traceable back to an impression. However, the sudden emergence—eruption—of imagination into the mix complicates matters. Does imagination *feel*? Does it—if imagination is indeed an "it"—merely carry this feeling of transition into the future? It surely cannot *know* which conjunctions are constant and which are not. It just as surely cannot discern, out of the innumerable impressions, which occur together constantly and which do not.

And the recourse to a natural instinct involves a circle just as surely as the presupposition that the future will resemble the past: we cannot render intelligible the origin of the idea of causality in nature either by reason or by experiment. (Fortunately!) nature has supplied us with instincts. Therefore, instincts will guide us where reason and experiment cannot. To bridge the "new impression" to the idea of causality by instinct is both understandable and ingenious. As we will soon see, it will open unanticipated promising vistas. But in retrospect, it falls far short of Hume's own standards of rigor.

The "new impression" of imagination is most peculiar, since it comes to our awareness *only upon reflection*. Yet it is at work all the time, and deserves the same respect as custom: it is most fully in operation when we are least aware of it. But considered strictly, we merely *call* the antecedent "cause" and the conception of its constant conjunct "effect." As Hume admits: "We have no idea of this notion [of cause], nor even any distinct notion what it is we desire to know, when we endeavour at a conception of it" (*EHU*, 77) Without this "new impression," we would not only lack the means to render our experience useful to us, we would also be unable to fathom even such fictions as cause and effect. We would not have anything that could be called *experience* at all. The distinction between impressions and ideas—what is its source? It cannot be an impression, nor can it be an idea. "Impressions" and "ideas" are no more and no less than *images* produced, held together, and held apart by imagination.[11] And natural instinct? This, too, is an image apart from the so-called impressions/ideas duality.

Impressions and ideas are both homogeneous and heterogeneous; to say this in another way, they *smear* in such a way that their distinguishability from one another both in general and in specific instances is often problematic. (Does feeling cold issue in the idea of vulnerability; or is it another "impression" of vulnerability, for example? Could it be both?) "Natural instinct," while said by Hume to be other, and to trump all abstract reasoning, is itself a product of abstract reasoning. At the very least, it follows reflection upon the failure of earlier abstract reasoning to establish its goal; still more, it accounts for what Hume calls our propensity to act even in the face of this failure. What is naturalism? It is an idea, or rather, a *very weak image* of Hume's thought.

What is called *experience* amounts to imaginal transitions, that is, to the flux of images to which we are given over. Imagination together with the flow of images is anterior to any determinations such as active/passive, subjective/objective, conscious/unconscious, etc., including impression/idea, and impulse/reason. Hume astutely locates what I will call collections of relative fixity within the flow. These may be called "guiding images," which are employed as means of negotiation within the flow. What, then, is the best that can be said for the idea of cause and effect? It is an *interpretation* of the flow of images that far exceeds not only description, but also explanation. It is not a "habit" in the Humean sense, but merely a repetition of what is contained in some of the very books that Hume would burn.

In order for Hume to remain a genuine Humean, another skeptical step must occur beyond the skeptical result of his inquiry into cause and effect. That step involves the reconciliation of language with the nature of imagery. Again, Socratic language and thought provide a model. The so-called (and miscalled) allegory of the cave and its aftermath provides the appropriate model as well as the appropriate way of recollection. After detailing the "underground cave-like dwelling" *(katageiō oikēsei spēlaiōdei)* (it is not called a cave) (514a) and its prisoners who have been chained facing the wall from childhood, Socrates hears Glaucon respond: "But this is a strange *(atopon)* image, and strange prisoners of which you speak." Socrates replies immediately, "they're like us" (515a). How are they "like us"? They are thoroughly bound to images. They mistake images for the things of which they are images. They have no notion as to whether the images and the sounds they hear emanate from anything behind them or not, if indeed they have any sense of "behind." They are closed off in principle from self-knowledge, having only the vaguest sense of self that is tied to their immediate perceptions—like us. One might say that they are Humeans who will never hear of Hume, while Socrates and Glaucon are Humeans.

Consider the liberation from the underground cavelike dwelling undergone by such a blind, image-bound person in terms only of his new "knowledge." First of all, he becomes aware of images for the first time. He had no hint concerning images at all. Gradually, he grows familiar with what can problematically be called "image/original" relations. I say problematically, since what is called "original" is found to be nothing other than a higher image. The highest of the images is the sun. It is highest not because it is grasped by the intellect alone, but because—in Humean language—it is *perceived* as providing illumination for all things on the earth. Socrates calls it a *cause,* but as we have seen, the Greek *aitia* and "cause" are not coextensive.

The commonality shared by Socrates, Glaucon, the underground men, and the liberated man is their bond to images, whether this bond is blind or not. The three major presentations by Socrates to Glaucon make this clear. In the first, the intellect is said to be an image—a child—of the good in what is called the intelligible region, and the sun serves as an image of the intellect in what is called the sensible region. These regions are strictly heterogeneous. The further image of yoking is brought forth in order to exhibit the connection between sight and the things seen and intellect and the things intellected. (Note the repeated twofolds in this first major image.) The second major image, the divided line, is both like and unlike the first. That is, it *images* the first. Like the first, the divided line indicates two regions, intelligible and sensible, which image one another. Unlike its predecessor, the two regions are imaged as *continuous,* that is, as homogeneous. Finally, the cave locates the human being as imprisoned in the sensible region and so as blindly ignorant of images (or of anything), but somehow as comfortable in these environs, unable to *imagine* any other. Force is necessary to remove a person from underground; pain and anger are the initial emotions at being so removed.

Once the liberated person has become accustomed, his progress is nothing less than amazing in every way. Where before he never questioned the reality of what passed on the wall before him, he now knows that they are images. And as he beholds the things around them, he becomes able to connect them somewhat as their source of his prior image-world. But as he contemplates himself and his new home, he slowly becomes aware that he remains anchored to what has previously been called the sensible region. In Socrates' speech from (508a–516b) in which he likens the ascent in knowledge on earth by the liberated person to the image of the divided line, he offers two striking disclaimers: "[O]nly a god knows if this happens to be true," and "[A]t least the appearances appear that way to me" (517b). That is, he opens up a distance in speech between the two images and collections of images. Now he knows that they were images and—if questioned closely after he has grown accustomed to life on the earth—he would say that he could now distinguish images from their so called "originals." That is, he is able to "see double" at once.

This double seeing has been prefigured in Book V, in the discussion that sets out to distinguish the philosopher from the lover of sights. In that discussion, Socrates presented three "tiers" of seers. The first seer acknowledges the existence of beautiful things but denies that there is such a thing as beauty itself. He is said to be asleep and in a dream, though he supposes that he is awake. The second seer is said to be "rare indeed," suggesting that this tier has no practitioners: this seer acknowledges the existence of beauty itself, but cannot see beautiful things. The third seer sees both beauty itself and beautiful things, and is cognizant of where one leaves off and the other begins. This seer is the only one said to be awake, though Socrates stops short of calling him "philosopher" (475e–476d).

But what can be said of these "originals"? Recalling the earlier discussion of *Phaedo* 100a–e in which "absolute beauty," "absolute goodness," and the like were shown in Socrates' own words to be *posits,* and in order to proceed from them they must be *granted* and *assumed.* To say it as directly as possible, there is no Theory of Ideas in Plato.[12] There are few passages that, taken completely out of context (e.g., the divided line), might seem to suggest something along those lines. But the widespread belief that Plato "held" such a theory is a testament to centuries of slipshod scholarship.

The divided line itself is continuous; the two so-called regions flow directly into one another. Read with due attention, the lowest rung, consisting of images in water and the like, are images of "things," the next lowest rung. The "things" are images of the lower rung of the (higher) intelligible region, namely hypotheses (in our terms, mathematical figures; Socrates calls them also "eidetic images"). The hypotheses, which can point downward to things in the sensible region, are themselves images of the *eidē*. "Form" is a dreadfully misleading translation of *eidos,* which is derived from *eidenai,* the past participle of *horaō,* an ordinary verb that means "to see." Its analogue under "affections of the soul" is similarly misleading: *nous* refers primarily to what we would call *perception* in a general sense, with an emphasis on what shows itself. The Platonic/Socratic "originals" are as far as possible from residing far from us on a lofty plane, accessible only to those capable of pure intellectual apprehension. Rather, they are *ruling images* that enable us to make sense of and navigate our way through our lives in the best manner available to us. (The central role of images in moral philosophy is rendered explicit from the outset in the second *Enquiry.*)

There is another kind of ruling image available to the one who pursues wisdom, or in other words, to the one for whom love of truth can never be excessive. This kind is available through inspired poetry. In *Republic* III, the passage in Homer's *Iliad* in which Achilles declares that he would rather be a slave on earth than be king of all the dead is censored from the education of the guardians "first of all" (386c). In the context of that education, the founders of the city in speech did not want this most celebrated hero depicted as hating death, as this depiction would instill fear of death in the guardians. But the guardians were not educated to pursue truth at all. Rather, truth to them was the inculcated opinion of what was good for the city.

However, the same passage that was censored "first of all" is said first of all to the person liberated from the cave (516d). In the latter context, the earth is preferred absolutely to the underground not because the liberated person fears death, but because the earth is the site that brings that person nearer the truth. The honors bestowed upon his former colleagues to the ones who are best able to "read" the shadows cannot be taken seriously but must be despised in comparison to whatever his new earthly home offers him. What does it offer? It offers genuine humanity. And what (among other things) does genuine humanity offer? Recognition of one's abiding ignorance or, to say the same thing in another manner, the capacity to see that one dwells amidst a play of images, to which one also belongs. The Homeric image shines out of the image play upon the image play from which it arises.

The Humean imagination-monitored flow of images most closely coheres with the results of his *Enquiry,* so long as these are *taken from his own words* and *follow from his own discourse.* The human understanding gives way to imagination: this is Hume's truly epoch-making insight. Is this an interpretation? Of course it is. But it is an interpretation that itself flows from the elements of the decisive move. The interpretation according to which we arrive at the idea of cause and effect from repeated constant conjunctions + subjective propensities, while not entirely incoherent, is a clumsy second-order account. It is entirely parasitical upon the flow of images and the occasional gatherings within that flow.

G. Aspects of Section IX: Of the Reason of Animals

This brief chapter seems to provide unequivocal support for the naturalist interpretation of Hume's thought. Like human beings, animals learn many things through the gradual accumulation of experience, following the same general principle "same 'causes,' same 'effects.'" Further, they do not use reason or argument to do so, any more than children do, than ordinary people do . . . or than philosophers do:

> It is custom alone, which engages animals, from every object, that strikes their senses, to infer its usual attendant, and carries their imagination, from the appearance of the one, to conceive the other, in that particular manner, which we denominate *belief*. (*EHU*, 106)

Different species obviously display different appearances and behaviors which are attributed to what Hume calls "the original hand of nature," governed by those instincts that so often engage our wonder. But, he claims, this "wonder will, perhaps, cease or diminish" (*EHU*, 108) once we recognize that our own human species operates in the same manner, namely by observation and experiment and by instincts and "mechanical power"—e.g., avoidance of bringing flesh and fire together—every bit as "natural" as the ones governing animals.

Leaving aside the earlier comments on the sudden and most peculiar notion of nature, of which we can have neither an impression nor an idea but which is somehow able to exercise those very causal properties belied by Hume's analysis, one can still call Hume an ancestor of Continental philosophy and a resource for it. Noteworthy first of all is the humbling of all human pretenses to superiority, aka Socratic ignorance. What credit can the most sapient human being take for her or his insight? Some, surely, but none that differs in kind from the most foolish. The efficiency of some animals in their performance of some tasks, such as "the art of incubation, and the whole economy and order of its nursery" (*EHU*, 108) of birds, exceeds ours.

Secondly, I say that it is false that our wonder diminishes once we grow aware that they operate according to what Hume calls "mechanical power." Once again, his own text works against this view. If we accept his stipulation that passions and sentiments are more powerful than reason, then it follows that our awareness of the mechanism of belief has a weaker influence upon us than the marvelous song of birds, the grace of swans, or the speed of cheetahs. These phenomena provide vivid perceptions that easily outstrip our epistemological insight. Finally, once we reinscribe the scruple concerning nature's strange "causality," we are returned to the flux of images that include those proximate that serve to guide our insight. That is, we do not find ourselves reasoning about causes, but rather we find ourselves interpreting phenomena.

Finally, it may be possible after all to inscribe a consistent notion of nature into Hume's text. Given the combination of nature's place in an epistemological no-man's land and its apparent at-hand-ness—in other words, given its opaque way of disclosure—we might regard it mythically, in the positive sense that *mythos* plays in the Platonic dialogues. That is, myth belongs to a certain way of showing in which matters crucial to human life although closed off to our knowledge may be brought to discourse. In the Platonic dialogues, death/immortality is one such abiding concern that does not receive much attention from Hume, and the little that it receives is almost entirely dismissive. However, nature—which would include death among its "properties"—certainly does.

In the early part of Plato's *Phaedrus,* there occurs a discussion of Socrates' nature in the context of myths within *mythos*. First, upon being asked by Phaedrus whether he would explain away the Boreas/Oreithyia myth in which the latter is swept away by the former by recourse to meteorology, Socrates claims to have no time for such activity and lets the myth stand. Then, he locates his own search for self-knowledge as dictated by the Delphic oracle within the myth of Typhon, the most hubristic monster of all who challenged Zeus for supremacy:

> Consequently I don't bother about [explaining myths away], but accept the current beliefs about them, and direct my inquiries, as I have just said, rather to myself, to discover whether I am a more complex creature and more puffed up with pride than Typhon, or a simpler, gentler being whom the gods have blessed with a quiet, un-Typhonic nature *(phusei)*. (230a)

"Nature" occurs here as both an inexplicable vertical granting from a heterogeneous source and as open to questioning, at least in the human realm. I suggest strongly that such an inscription, while alien to Hume's language, is entirely in keeping with the results of his first *Enquiry* in a way that his own discourse on nature contravenes it. Socratic "nature" surpasses our knowledge, and is discovered rather than given. Wonder is preserved even as its specific workings are disclosed. The "mechanical power" is its least interesting feature.

H. Aspects of Section XII: Of the Academical or Sceptical Philosophy

What do we know concerning external objects? We know that we do not perceive external objects directly. This is clear because of the differences that ensure when we modify our distance from them. Nor do we perceive images of external objects. There is no pathway through the image to the object that is supposedly imaged. Regarding external objects, we know nothing:

> This is a topic, therefore, in which the profounder and more philosophical sceptics will always triumph, when they endeavour to introduce a universal doubt into all subjects of human knowledge and enquiry. Do you follow the instincts and propensities of nature, may they say, in assenting to the veracity of sense? But these lead you to believe that the very perception or sensible image is the external object. Do you disclaim this principle, in order to embrace a more rational opinion, that the perceptions are only representations of something external? You here depart from your natural propensities and more obvious sentiments; and yet are not able to satisfy your reason, which can never find any convincing argument from experience to prove, that the perceptions are connected with any external objects. (*EHU*, 153–54)

The full light of reason, according to Hume, "borders upon the most profound darkness. And between [what she illuminates and what she finds dark] she is so dazzled and confounded, that she scarcely can pronounce with certainty and assurance concerning any one object" (*EHU*, 157). As Hume notes, if one could actually perform Cartesian radical doubt (an impossibility in principle), one could never extricate oneself from it. If this chapter is read straightforwardly and with even the most superficial care, its conclusion is that Pyrrhonism—or what Hume calls "excessive skepticism"—is the *truth*.

A major difficulty, however, arises in loving truth with the passion Hume has earlier exempted from censure of any kind: it would lead to utter sloth, indifference, and gradual death. But it does not: "nature," which—whatever it is—"is always too strong for principle" (*EHU*, 160), enters where reason breaks off. As a result, such philosophical passion-for-truth is assigned by Hume to the schools alone! A question arises—suddenly?—when the truth comes out of hiding: "We need only ask such a sceptic, *What his meaning is? And what he proposes by all these curious researches?* He is immediately at a loss, and knows not what to answer" (*EHU*, 159–60). But this is disingenuous, and perhaps deliberately so.

The three virtues of the abstruse philosophy were listed in the first section: its service to the easy philosophy, its infusion of the spirit of accuracy into all fields, and the gratification of intellectual curiosity. First of all, there is no doubt that Hume is "such a sceptic." Further, the latter three virtues give a clear answer to both questions. So, to take a step back, let it be asked: From whence come these questions, or from whom? Recall the irreconcilable disparity between being an abstruse philosopher and being a man. When the two are joined, the result is "some strange uncouth monster" (*THN*, 264). These questions, in the context provided by the final section of the first *Enquiry*, issue from the side of the "man" who has no interest in abstruse philosophy but who enjoys the comforts and the appearance of erudition belonging to bourgeois life.

It would be mistaken to call the Humean condition schizophrenia either in the psychiatric sense or the more literal sense of a state in which there is a split in the *phrenes*. For Hume, there simply is no separable *phrenes*. In one of his many delightfully playful passages, he declares that unlike some misguided metaphysicians, all other human beings regard each individual self as "nothing but a bundle or collection of different perceptions" (*THN*, 252), hardly a likely result of a poll taken even in that more enlightened age. He calls the mind "a kind of theatre," but almost at once retracts this likeness:

> The comparison of the theatre must not mislead us. [The perceptions] are the successive perceptions only, that constitute the mind; nor have we the most distant notion of the place, where these scenes are represented, or of the materials, of which it is compos'd. (*THN*, 253)

Another non sequitur, this one consisting of deriving continued existence and identity of the mind from continued perception, accounts for belief in this particular fiction. Once again, imagination makes the leap precisely at the point where reason can go no farther—or perhaps more precisely, imagination has always already made that leap.

However, Hume not only answered to his name, but wrote a short, charming, and deceptively profound biography near his death titled "My Own

Life," written in the first person. It catalogues his disappointments and his satisfactions, and records the favorable responses from friends and his few foes alike to his agreeable, moderate disposition. It is what might be called a splendid and persuasive fiction—not unlike the one by which we ascribe a personal identity to ourselves and others in spite of its theoretical impossibility. Returning to the peculiar offering/withdrawing of the image of the mind as theatre-like, in "My Own Life" Hume is both image and image maker. Hume thinks himself as the stage of the play he has written, with the characters drawn broadly and generally with those whom he encountered on the way—including his own. Quite remarkably, he presents his "own life," at least on its surface, as blameless.

This self-doubling of Hume recalls Plato's *Second Letter*, albeit in a peculiar way. In the latter, Plato writes that he will publish no philosophy in his own name, but will present "a Socrates made beautiful and new."[13] This peculiar authorial doubling produces some strikingly anomalous developments. In the *Phaedo*, where the "absence" of its author is noted in its text and where Socrates presents his most extensive (though also brief) account of his own life, an apparent disparity between parts of Socrates' *logos* and his *erga* are exposed. One noteworthy example: Socrates speaks of the soul's imprisonment in the body, and of death as if it were a release from this imprisonment. The practice of philosophy, since philosophy is putatively directed toward the apprehension of the pure *eidē* by pure *nous*, is practice for death. But before the outset of his entire discourse as reported by Phaedo, he makes a point of placing his bare feet on the earth and of practicing music as directed by a dream. At its end, he sings a "swan song" not of the heavens where the disembodied soul would supposedly dwell but *of the earth.*

There is no schizophrenic Socrates either, but in a somewhat different sense: the Socrates of the dialogues is an authorial construction, an *image,* or—in Humean terms—a fiction of the imagination. However, like the bifurcated Hume who serves both as image maker and image, the Socrates of the dialogues is written as also both image maker and image. If we were to look at both through the lens of the Humean theoretical "self," both Hume and Socrates come to appear only through their perceptions—and through our own continuous perceptions of them. Apart from these, one cannot locate an identical Socrates, or an identical Plato, or an identical Hume beyond these perceptions. In the most important sense, these three thinkers offer us vicarious participation in madness and monstrosity, that is, they offer a glimpse into who and what we are at the deepest level. Only secondarily do they provide "doctrines," if indeed they really do so at all.

From *An Enquiry Concerning Human Understanding* to *An Enquiry Concerning the Principles of Morals*

It requires no great insight to observe the difference between *An Enquiry Concerning Human Understanding* and *An Enquiry Concerning the Principles of Morals*. The former is characterized by skepticism, at least in the theoretical realm, while the latter seems to have no trace of it. What unites the two? "Human nature," we are told, which is the "primitive element [of both], beyond which explanation cannot go."[14] Perhaps "explanation" cannot reach beyond human nature, but *description*—at least description of a certain sort—can surely be supplied. Hume writes within the limits of his tradition. In the second *Enquiry*, we find him discussing the foundations of morality in terms of reason and sentiment, much as we found him delineating his mental geography in terms of matters of fact and relations of ideas in the first *Enquiry*.

Before discussing this difference, however, it will prove useful to sketch a pathway from the first *Enquiry* to the second in terms of what may seem like a marked shift to contemporary eyes, but which shows itself to be far less dramatic in light of Platonic underpinnings. The word *logos* does a great deal of work in its Greek context: indeed, "word" is its primary sense. Though the usual translation into English is "argument," this word does not appear until quite late in the very large collection of senses given in *LSJ*, and long after *"mythos,"* one of its earliest identifications. Identified by Aristotle as the preferred rhetorical means (the others are *pathos* and *ethos*), its characterization as "rational discourse" as opposed to emotional and moral appeals yield our dominant sense of *logos* as *argument*. Aristotle calls deductive argument that produces a certain kinds of knowledge a *demonstration (apodeixis)* or proof. A demonstration is "a syllogism productive of scientific knowledge."[15] However, the "arguments" of the first *Enquiry* appear to be much tighter than those in the second. As we have seen, and as Hume notes, its skeptical arguments seem in their soundness to undermine the efficacy of rational argumentation itself to establish truth, even of the most apparently obvious kind (*EHU*, 155–56). In other words, they are *proofs* that establish Hume's theoretical skepticism on rational grounds.

However, there is an older and different sense of demonstration or proof that can be found at a turning point of Plato's *Phaedrus*. *Apodeixis*, from *apo-deiknumi (apo-deiknumi)*, means "to show from," strictly speaking. Reading it as proof in the sense of "rational argument" is to impose a later interpretation upon it in terms of a logical/scientific orientation. *Mythos* was, in an earlier period (and in this dialogue written by Plato, his teacher) a suitable way of *apodeixis*. Just before launching onto his second *logos*, his great myth of the soul, Socrates tells Phaedrus, "This *apodeixis* will not be trusted by the clever *(deinois)* on the one hand, but on the other hand the wise ones *(sophois)* will trust it" (245c). As we will soon see, the basis of the argumentation in the second *Enquiry* lies closer to this earlier sense of *apodeixis*.

No one would equate Hume's discourse to Socrates' great myth. However, there is also one astonishing aspect that, in a distant but meaningful analogy, presages a key development in Hume's second *Enquiry*. I refer to the special place of *beauty*.

In the great myth, the immortal soul has, once upon a time in its disembodied travels, beheld the train of the gods as they took their places at the divine banquet, where from the edge of the heavens they feasted on "being beingly being *(ousia ontōs ousa)*" (247c). In their journey, human souls have

> witnessed a blest sight and spectacle, and we were initiated into what is lawful to call the most blest of the mysteries. Celebrating these inspired rites, we were whole and untouched by those evils which lay in wait for us later. Being fully initiated and looking upon whole, simple, unchanging and blessed visions *(phasmata)* in pure light, we were ourselves pure and untouched by what we now carry around and call a body, a thing which imprisons us like an oyster shell, that were perfect, and simple, and unshakeable and blissful . . . and we saw it in pure light because we were pure ourselves . . . ." (250b–c)

The tradition of Plato scholarship regards these as the Ideas, but it is crucial to note that they are (1) suggested here in the context of a myth, and as more recent and more thoughtful Plato interpretation has shown, (2) they never occur as objects of a theory nor are they ever invoked as actually seen. Still further, they are called *phasmata,* "things that come to light." More to the point here, however, is that only beauty among the "blessed *phasmata*" is apprehensible to us embodied humans, as it alone comes through vision, the sharpest of our bodily senses.

Though the analogy may appear distant, I strongly suggest the presence of a deep kinship between the Platonic notion of beauty's uniqueness in the embodied human region and Hume's notion of the immediate pleasure to human beings that utility tenders. Beauty in the human region provokes the recollection of the divine banquet, where being shone most brightly. Socrates' depiction of the passionately chaste *erōs* provoked by the beauty of a boy and the way this *erōs* is enacted in philosophical conversation is imaged in the pleasure taken in benevolence and its allied qualities and—more to the point here—in utility.

Hume has declared the futility of seeking reasons for qualities of our humanity that are immediately manifest:

> It is needless to push our researches so far as to ask, why we have humanity or a fellow-feeling with others. It is sufficient, that this is experienced to be a principle in human nature. We must stop somewhere in our examination of causes; and there are, in every science, some general principles, beyond which we cannot hope to find any principle more general. No man is absolutely indifferent to the happiness and misery of others. The first has a *natural tendency* to give pleasure; the second, pain. This every one may find in himself. . . . But if it were possible, it belongs not to the present subject; and we may here safely consider these principles as original: happy, if we can render all the consequences sufficiently plain and perspicuous! (*EPM,* 219n–20n; emphasis mine)

Hume's apparently non-mythical "natural tendency toward pleasure" images the Platonic mythical "blessed vision of beauty" that was ours before we became embodied, at which point we were given over then to the mixture of pleasures and pains that each of us experiences. I contend that neither Hume nor Plato believed in knowledge beyond that which comes through "experience" or "human vision." Hume's skepticism regarding causes echoes Socrates' dismissal of those causes putatively belonging to natural science *(phusikē epistēmē),* accepting the legitimacy of the eidetic cause (misleadingly rendered as "formal cause") alone. Hume would not admit the eidetic as a cause proper; his interest (though critical) is in the efficient cause (theoretically), and, in a way, in the telic or final cause ("all the consequences!" as gathered in it) morally, namely the happiness of humankind.

Chapter II

Aspects of *An Enquiry Concerning the Principles of Morals*

Unlike his first *Enquiry* in particular, his second *Enquiry* takes place primarily on the plane of *imagery*. It takes its departure from a single insight:

> Let a man's insensibility be ever so great, he must often be touched with the *images* of *Right* and *Wrong*; and let his prejudices be ever so obstinate, he must observe, that others are susceptible of like impressions. (*EPM*, 170; emphasis mine)

Its journey consists primarily of encomiums to the moral virtues and of many images drawn from poetry, history, literature, and everyday life. He certainly offers cogent arguments as well. But unlike those in the first *Enquiry*, here they tend both to repeat and to rely far more on persuasive language than their counterparts in its apparently more radical predecessor. While it is no longer entirely unnoticed, its "incomparable" character has remained largely unobserved, however one regards Hume's judgment of it. In the scholarship, it has been treated almost exclusively as a moral disquisition much like others, that is, as primarily offering a series of arguments that lead to conclusions involving universality, sentiment, reason, pleasure, oneself, society, etc. One could spend days in a well-stocked library and never read a word about what makes this book quite obviously different from all of his other works.

There are two plain reasons why the second *Enquiry* receives, by comparison to its predecessor, relatively little attention in our era. First of all, Hume's unapologetically expressed views are sexist and racist by today's more enlightened standards, not even to mention his "principled" contempt even for imaginary beings who are rational but weaker than we are. Examples abound concerning women, but this one alone from an argument against the soul's immortality should suffice:

> On the theory of the soul's mortality, the inferiority of women's capacity is easily accounted for. Their domestic life requires no higher faculties either of mind or body. This circumstance vanishes and becomes absolutely insignificant on the religious theory: the one sex has an equal task to perform as the other; their powers of reason and resolution ought also to have been equal . . .[1]

The contemporary author who cites this passage writes: "The argument is archaic. As with Hume's (or Kant's, or Aristotle's) sexist and racist remarks elsewhere, one is left wondering why he (or Kant, or Aristotle) could not see through the prejudices of his age."[2] Given the voluminous history of great minds expressing incongruously small and vicious prejudices, perhaps this task is not quite so easy or straightforward. As Hume and Socrates, our two main thinkers here, teach, a significant measure of blindness belongs to all of us.

For a racist statement, in which he criticizes his peers for their treatment of "inferiors," Hume writes:

> [Restraint in the use of superior power] is plainly the situation of men, with regard to animals; and how far these may be said to possess reason, I leave it to others to determine. The great superiority of civilized Europeans above barbarous Indians, tempted us to imagine ourselves on the same footing with regard to them, and made us throw off all restraints of justice, and even of humanity, in our treatment of them. (*EPM*, 191)

Regarding those imaginary rational beings who are weaker than we are, Hume advises:

> Our intercourse with them could not be called society, which supposes a degree of equality; but absolute command on the one side, and servile obedience on the other. Whatever we covet, they must instantly resign: Our permission is the only tenure, by which they hold their possessions: Our compassion and kindness the only check, by which they curb our lawless will: And as no inconvenience ever results from the exercise of a power, so firmly established in nature, the restraints of justice and property, being totally *useless*, would never have place in so unequal a confederacy. (*EPM*, 190–91)

Mindful of the high price paid and noble sacrifices made by so many (rights activists both famous and anonymous, and opponents of tyranny who continue to court danger as they press for justice) one may surely take issue with Hume's claim that significantly weaker beings reside below any claim of justice. As an apology for Hume on this matter, I appeal to another great philosopher known for incendiary remarks, Friedrich Nietzsche, whose decontextualized remarks against virtually every nation, group, gender, religion, etc., make him appear monstrous indeed—almost as monstrous as he wished to appear.

In Nietzsche's early *On the Uses and Disadvantages of History for Life* (1874), he distinguishes three kinds of history and three kinds of uses/disadvantages. The most measured—one might say the most harmless, though nothing pertaining to life can be entirely harmless—is antiquarian history. The antiquarian historian serves life by piously preserving what is best from the past and so handing it down to future generations as their ever-ongoing heritage. However, it both falsifies the past by highlighting only certain selections, and does not engender life but merely comments upon it. As such, it can do neither great good nor great harm.

Monumental history, however, serves life by providing models for the most vital of human beings; it is necessary for the highest life in that the accomplishment of great deeds of the past gives surety to the possibility of great deeds in the present. However, the attempt to build something great is both subject to dangerous excess and may be destructive of life in certain cases, namely when an ungrounded mythology replaces healthy vital need and when fanaticism is inflamed by this impulse.

By contrast, critical history serves life by throwing off the burden of the past for the sake of creating new values in the present. Like monumental history, it can do great good and great harm, but the similarity ends there. In critical history, the past is held up to the standards of the present and—justly or not—is found wanting against this standard and often obliterated entirely. Often it affirms the gains humanity has made, and promises still greater ones. The danger is that in cutting off the past, it cuts off our origins and our roots, together with the flaws that belong to who and what we are. Nietzsche here recommends a discipline by which the past is not eliminated but is rather the formation of a "second nature" built upon the past with the aid of the life-giving critical history.

Here, as is often the case, monumental history and critical history are at odds. As a critical historian, I must categorically condemn Hume's aforementioned beliefs. However, as a monumental historian, I must affirm Hume's moral philosophy as a great deed that is necessarily worth preserving and emulating. In addition, the principles it advances undermine the particular prejudiced judgments he makes in putative accord with them, some of which will make even the most retrograde contemporary reader wince. It is my view, however, that modern philosophy, despite the time-bound views of its authors (e.g., Hume, Kant, Hegel), has provided the most powerful means for their overcoming. I will treat this issue from time to time in what follows.

Further, *An Enquiry Concerning the Principles of Morals* presupposes a degree of classical learning in its readers that is all but entirely absent today. Although most editions give these references in footnotes, they require contextualization in order to gather their sense within the text. There must be a scholar *somewhere* who loves Hume, who can absorb Hume's outdated prejudices with aplomb, and who possesses the erudition that is required to provide a variorum edition of this wonderful and important book. In the meantime, I will attempt to supply a few readings of philosophical consequence where they seem germane.

In any case, those scholars who maintain that the second *Enquiry* merely recasts the results of the third section of the *Treatise* ("of Morals") in a more accessible way are, quite simply, wrong on every count. The second *Enquiry* is *less* accessible, not more. It is less accessible precisely because of the playfulness that occurs on every page, recalling the playfulness of the Platonic dialogues of which John Sallis has said: "This is to say that the interpreter must become—though in a different way—one of the interlocutors of the dialogue."[3] This holds for Hume's *Enquiry,* in which the reader is often addressed directly and with smiles of many kinds.

Just as in the first *Enquiry,* however, Hume's language is unable to contain the depths of his thought. Human nature is inextricably bound with madness and delirium, that is, with intersystematic contradictions that can neither be avoided nor reconciled. The passivity of reason carries over from the *Treatise* and the first *Enquiry*. However, without sustained and intricate chains of reasoning, the sentiments cannot be properly moved to moral action. The sentiments are already disposed toward morality, if only in the minimal sense indicated above. Of course they are also disposed toward mere selfishness. What would be required in order to realize Hume's suspicion "that *reason* and *sentiment* concur in almost all moral determinations and conclusions" (*EPM,* 172)? It will require a monstrous act of imagination.

Concerning his procedure, Hume appears to follow a standard empiricist line and denounce his "rationalist" opponents:

> As [the assignment of praise or blame to moral qualities] this is a question of fact, not of abstract science, we can only expect success, by following the experimental method, and deducing general maxims from a comparison of particular instances. The other scientific method, where a general abstract principle is first established, and

is afterwards branched out into a variety of inferences and conclusions, may be more perfect in itself, but suits less the imperfection of human nature and is a common source of illusion and mistake in this as well as in other subjects. (*EPM*, 174)

However, the support for this method comes from "the nature of language," rather than from any matter of fact. "Good" and "bad," estimable and blamable, have the same cross-linguistic meaning. The experiment then, is to discern those qualities that are universally called "good," and those that are universally called "bad." Having done so, we may determine the principles of morals.

Several responses to this arise from this innocuous beginning. First of all, "deduce" simply means "infer" in a very loose sense—there is no hint of its meaning in logic. The sense of "general" is ambiguous—generality can be relative, but need not be. But what can one say about "universal"? The "nature of language" dictates that there can be no exceptions. The question, then, is the following: How can the experimental method be reconciled with a notion of the nature of language such that imputations of "estimable" and "blamable" are the same within every human breast? I do not believe that the author of the first *Enquiry* could be capable of fashioning such a messy argument. Rather, his insight must be relocated away from the language of general, particular, and universal to the language of *imagery* with which the second *Enquiry* began.

It is clear that a single exception to Hume's criterion of imputation would sink his argument, and one would not have to look far to find such an exception. However, the model for Hume's method here is neither "natural philosophy" (the natural sciences) nor is it the skeptical method that he employed in the first *Enquiry*. Rather, *exhibition* and *description* are two words that distinguish this method from the others. It would not stretch matters at all to say that these means present themselves under the sway of a certain *musicality*. Many of Hume's citations suggest Clio (especially), Euterpe, and even Erato; further, Hume's prose in the second *Enquiry* fairly sings. We behold a series of vicarious images. As we will see, the reasoning (such as it is) serves primarily to support the images.

Of Benevolence

Part I

Hume begins this section with an assertion that seems false on its face, namely, that what he calls "the benevolent or softer affections" have pride of place among the moral virtues. Their virtual synonyms include:

> [t]he epithets *sociable, good-natured, humane, merciful, grateful, friendly, generous, beneficent,* or their equivalents, [which] are known in all languages, and universally express the highest merit, which *human nature* is capable of attaining. (*EPM*, 176)

Looking at this first paragraph as an argument, it is a particularly wretched one: shining achievement and/or exceptional wealth produce envy, but when these qualities are coupled with humaneness and beneficence, even the envious will forgo their jealousy and applaud their bearer. This is simply not so.

To buttress this dubious claim—if it is, indeed, a claim—Hume (loosely) cites Plutarch's account (Plutarch in *Pericle* 38) of the famous final words of Pericles, who had heard the praises of his friends who surrounded him:

> "*You forget,* cries the dying hero, who had heard all, *you forget the most eminent of my praises, while you dwell so much on those vulgar advantages, in which fortune had a principal share. You have not observed that no citizen has ever yet worne mourning on my account.*"
> (EPM, 177)

How strong is this "premise"? Plutarch's dates are AD 46–120; Pericles' are 495–429 BC, or five hundred years earlier. Plutarch has also been known to embellish his accounts. Further, Pericles remained a controversial figure even after his death, although we speak today of Athens' golden age as "the age of Pericles." Finally, it is not true, strictly speaking, that no citizen had mourned on account of Pericles. While there is no evidence of his having taken anyone's life by his own hand, his confident launch of the Greek strategy in the early years of the Peloponnesian War, while somewhat successful, led to the deaths of many Athenian citizens; in one period he was even ostracized. Further, the generally favorable historical judgment of him rests ultimately on his great political wisdom and his oratory skills, and not on his beneficence. Finally, Pericles' praise of himself hardly proves the superiority of his humaneness over his other "glorious" virtues. Two further *ad verecundiam* passages follow, one citing Cicero, in which the softer virtues restrain more ambitious characters, and the other from Juvenal, in which these virtues can be more widely spread if they occur in persons of high rank.

Given the unprecedented acuity and precision of Hume's argumentation in the first *Enquiry,* what are we to make of this flaccid performance? The first sentence of the following paragraph offers a most suggestive clue:

> But I forget, that it is not my present business to recommend generosity and benevolence, or to paint, in their true colours, all

the genuine charms of the social virtues. These, indeed, sufficiently engage every heart, on the first apprehension of them; and it is difficult to abstain from some sally or panegyric. . . . But our object here [is] more the speculative, than the practical part of morals . . . (*EPM*, 177–78)

"Panegyric," from the Greek *panēgyrikos* meaning an oration of or for a festival assembly, became restricted to funerals under the Romans but here finds itself employed in a most vital sense. Hume, of course, did not forget anything—if he had, the aforementioned passages would have been excised. Such playful absence of restraint echoes Socrates' final speech in *Republic* I, in which Socrates likens himself to a glutton for pursuing arguments for the goodness (versus the badness) of justice before determining what the just is.

It is tempting to say that Hume's Part I serves to establish the *agreeableness* of the aforementioned softer affections by means of images that will appeal immediately to the reader, while the anchoring theoretical arguments will be reserved for the second section. However, these images always involve a competition between ambitious qualities that are, according to the historians, mitigated to some degree by the softer ones. One can easily provide cases in which a softer response is highly problematic. It is surely too much to say that Hume's examples are immediately—unequivocally—pleasing. There must be more to this.

Part II

The panegyric continues. The humane, beneficent man (presumably having a measure of social status), in bestowing the blessings of these qualities upon all who fall within his influence, is said to be "[l]ike the sun, an inferior minister of providence, [who] cheers, invigorates, and sustains the surrounding world" (*EPM*, 178). Since these qualities, whether public or private, enjoy universal approval, Hume concludes that "utility . . . forms, at least, a *part* of their merit" (*EPM*, 179).

What are offered as premises? A secondhand account by Cicero in which the Epicurean gods deserve no worship on account of their uselessness, rendering them even worse than Egyptian animal worship. The assertion by Sextus Empiricus that religious worship originated from the usefulness of inanimate objects such as the sun and the moon (however absurd this notion); also the reason for deification of heroes and legislators of great merit. We are no nearer to "speculative" concerns than we were in Part I.

From these examples, Hume "concludes" that determinations of morality can be made with no greater certainty than by "ascertaining, on any side, the true interests of mankind" (*EPM*, 180). He adds that further experience and better reasoning can lead us to adjust our views in light of them. This view has the positive result of subjecting Hume's racism, sexism, and colonialism to reevaluation. However, it seems to be guilty of the same self-acknowledged piggishness of Socrates at the end of *Republic* I: the prior question, namely what *are* the true interests of mankind, has not been raised. Thus far, they seem to be determined by a scantily presented cross-linguistic agreement between cultures, by highly selective appeals to authority, and by a false proposition concerning the universal applause received by the gentler sentiments. One need only recall the strident and hostile epithets heaped upon members of the American citizenry who had the temerity to oppose its recently many and ill-conceived wars, where the alternative of rational argument was clearly at hand. Nor was the eighteenth-century British Commonwealth a scene of praise without exception for the softer qualities.

What then? Then we must follow the thread in Hume that regards the philosophical apprehension of morals as an *entirely human* phenomenon, unlike philosophical (theoretical) speculation that can offer arguments which lead to an incontrovertible conclusion. It would be ridiculous to claim that Hume's disclosure of the circularity belonging to any argument for efficient causality in the first *Enquiry* applies to only a part of causality, or to some causes but perhaps not others. But as "morals" to Hume has a sense that bridges not only reason and sentiment but individual actions and social actions, the relative looseness of his presentations accords with the nature of his subject matter. One perhaps hears an Aristotelian echo from the *Nichomachean Ethics,* according to which the degree of precision depends upon the nature of the subject matter.

Rethinking Hume's account in terms suitable to contemporary Continental philosophy, Hume does not offer arguments at all, but *image-play coupled with aids for its beholding.* That is, in order to be taken up properly his discourse must be approached *aesthetically;* the aids may be regarded as helpful guides to the images in this "incomparable" gallery. The Platonic restriction of human knowledge to images once again makes itself manifest in Hume's playful/serious thought. In these terms, his chapter on benevolence (and Hume himself) might be called *kalos te kai agathos,* beautiful and good. The elegance of his prose and his deployment of appropriate citations within it draw one toward his "claim." But what is this claim? It is nothing other than our knowledge of what the words *good* and *beautiful,* or *right* and *wrong,* already contain in any language prelinguistically, that is, as they derive from images inscribed in the human heart.[4]

What do we already know, and where does this knowledge find its limit? We know what the words *right* and *wrong* mean; applying these meanings in human affairs is quite a different matter, and requires a kindred awareness of measure. Certain actions that seem to partake of benevolence can have pernicious outcomes. Giving alms to beggars seems admirable, but leads to "idleness and debauchery" (*EPM*, 180). Tyrannicide rids a nation of a monster, but often leads to "the jealousy and cruelty of princes" (*EPM*, 180–81). Even luxury, which satirists and moralists condemn as unequivocally evil, has its virtuous side: the desire for luxuries increases not only industriousness but artistic, political, (and even moral) practices. Thus, our prior knowledge of right and wrong does not sufficiently provide *principles,* that is, universal rules, of morals. Hume's discussion of the aforementioned practices, which concludes with their moral indeterminacy, demonstrates this insufficiency. It resembles nothing so much as a kind of Socratic questioning, a modern *elenchus*. The result—concerning giving alms, tyrannicide, and luxury—is *aporia*.

The word *aretē*, usually translated as *virtue*, connotes a positive quality; its opposite, *kakia*, is more variously translated—e.g., sometimes as *badness*, sometimes as *evil,* sometimes as *vice*. The connotation is always negative. Hume's images of right and wrong map quite well onto their ancient Greek correlates. In Plato's *Meno,* we find a kindred investigation and kindred tendencies. Meno begins by asking how virtue is acquired: by nature (i.e., by physical birth)? by teaching? by practice? in some other way? In a relatively long, ironic response which seems to wander far from Meno's question, Socrates indicates that until he knows what virtue *is,* he is in no position to engage the question of how it might be acquired.

For our purposes, it is enough to note that beyond Meno's obtuseness, two matters of interest present themselves. (1) There is an equivocation in the sense of *aretē*. It can mean something along the lines *of moral goodness;* it can also mean *virtuosity,* exceptional skill. Achilles drags the carcass of Hector through the dirt: one can say that Achilles is both virtuous as a warrior in having vanquished his enemy and unvirtuous in outraging the protocols of warfare. Socrates speaks of virtue almost always as moral goodness; this causes some (though hardly all) of Meno's confusion. (2) In speaking of virtue as moral goodness, Socrates presumes that every interlocutor will understand him; in other words, that there is indeed a shared sense—or image—of virtue to which he can always appeal.

This is most apparent in Meno's third answer to the question "What is virtue?" "To rejoice in beautiful things and in power" (77b). Socrates proceeds to refute both parts of Meno's answer by presupposing the "moral goodness" sense of virtue. Bad men as well as good men rejoice in beautiful things, and power can be used for good and for bad. Meno concurs—at least in speech. He concurs in the "moral goodness" sense of virtue, at least tacitly. Also, he admits to confusion *(aporia)*. However, he attributes his confusion to the famous Socratic sting that has struck otherwise sagacious Meno dumb,[5] rather than to his own lack of insight.

As Hume's text proceeds, however, one cannot help but notice a gradual and nuanced overlay of the more ancient sense of virtue that Meno's third answer suggests when he claims that "to have power" *(dunasthai)* (77b) belongs to it. As we take departure from Hume's panegyric to the softer virtues, we shall note the advent of some of the harsher ones.

Of Justice

Part I

The limits of justice—or rather, the limits within which justice appears—are set by what Hume calls *fictions,* but which I would call *vicarious images*. We live through the first, the poetical fiction, by imagining the "profuse *abundance* of all *external* conveniences" (*EPM,* 183), a situation in which justice could not appear. Every individual lives unclothed due to the clemency of the seasons, and is well fed by the delicious and healthful fare offered by nature.

> No laborious occupation required: no tillage: no navigation. Music, poetry, and contemplation form his sole business: conversation, mirth, and friendship his sole amusement. (*EPM,* 182)

Such external plenty would have the same salubrious influence on each individual's internal state. Since there is more than enough of everything for everyone, individual property would not be contested, and conflicts concerning what is *mine* and what is *thine* could not occur. Thus, no justice appears—because in such a circumstance, justice would be useless.

The second fiction, the philosophical fiction, presents a vicarious image of relentless belligerence, the result of the lack of the most basic requirements for human life. This fiction of the so-called state of nature "is painted out as a state of mutual war and violence, attended by the most extreme necessity" (*EPM,* 189). As a result of its uselessness under such circumstances, justice would also not appear. The two fictions are, of course similar in major respects: in them, there is found no law, no property, no need to reach agreements—hence, no justice. Hume extends the philosophical fiction farther when he imagines the plight of "a virtuous man" who finds himself suddenly in the midst of "such barbarians":

He, meanwhile, can have no other expedient than to arm himself, to whomever the sword he seizes, or the buckler, may belong. . . . And his particular regard to justice being no longer of use to his own safety or that of others, he must consult the dictates of self-preservation alone, without concern for those who no longer merit his care and attention. (*EPM,* 187)

The images attendant to the poetical and philosophical fictions in what might be called their pure forms require a corresponding more or less pure act of imagination, as no one of us has ever encountered either state—as in the city in speech of Plato's *Republic,* no philosophy could occur. *Philo-sophia* can only occur when *need* occurs, when some discord appears that calls for questioning. Hume's addendum to the philosophical fiction adds an element of recognition that is absent from the pure form. Whether on an individual or political scale, sudden eruptions of cruel and lawless disorder thrust otherwise "virtuous" people into exceptional circumstances where the rules of justice no longer obtain. A woman who plunges a knife into a man's stomach has committed a criminal injustice if there are no mitigating circumstances. If the man is in the act of attacking her sexually, the same action is blameless, even heroic. The current resistance to the lawless and predatory Mugabe government in Zimbabwe is similarly just and praiseworthy. This is one clear complication issuing from the earlier unconditional celebration of the "softer" virtues.

Still another complication arises from a third image, distinct both in nature and in form from the previous ones. This image has already been presented above, and concerns a fictive race of beings much like ourselves with respect to rationality, but qualitatively weaker than we are. With what can sound very much like heartless cruelty in our age in which animal suffering is a concern and animal rights has become a significant branch of philosophy, Hume maintains that the bonds of justice between us and such beings would not obtain *at all.* (He does say, in a gesture to our softer side, that kindness toward such beings would not be *prima facie* blameworthy.)

Like his great successor Kant, who honors him both in word and in deed more than does any other thinker, Hume is a poor Plato scholar—who nevertheless reconfigures some of Plato's key elements in fateful ways. Hume misreads Books II–IV of the *Republic,* calling these books a refutation of a conception of the "state of nature" much older than Hobbes's conception (*EPM,* 189n). The Platonic city in speech is rather a civilized city, but whose inhabitants have designs on luxuries that can only be secured through warfare.[6]

In Book V, upon which Hume has no comment here, Adeimantus and Glaucon accuse Socrates of "robbing us of a whole *eidos* of the *logos.*" Its conclusion, namely that the citizens of the purified city in speech will forgo all individual ownership, receives strong challenge:

> And you supposed you would have escaped notice, as though it were something quite trivial, that after all it's plain to everyone that, concerning women and children, the things of friends will be in common. (449c)

With this challenge, Socrates admits that it provokes myriad complications, the first two of which have their source in the "sudden" advent of *erōs*, which was banned from the city in speech. Socrates can only offer hope that his interlocutors will not heap ridicule upon him. Women are to exercise naked along with the men, who will see them "clothed in virtue rather than robes" (457a). Since erotic necessities can be "more stinging" (458d) than geometric necessities, matings must be strictly regulated and managed so that "the best men have intercourse as often as possible with the best women" (459d). This comedy, in which *erōs* is treated as if it could be made subject to human manipulation, provides a more fanciful image than does the city in speech in which all desires are made subject to calculation allied with spirit.

As in the first four books of the *Republic*, *erōs* is absent from all of Hume's fictions. However, sexuality certainly is not. It makes an initial appearance here, where Hume speaks of

> the conjunction of the sexes to be established in nature, [from which] a family immediately arises; and particular rules being found requisite for its subsistence, these are immediately embraced; though without comprehending the rest of mankind within their prescriptions. (*EPM*, 192)

I suggest that here, perhaps disingenuously, Hume has introduced another "poetical fiction" in which one can discover the seed of justice in some imaginary instinctive nuclear family operating under instinctive rules for the good of all its members. Such "rules" have historically included the subjugation of women, and one trembles at some possible contemporary feminist response to this fiction.[7] One effect of Hume's time-bound belief in the inequality of women is the distortion—or more neutrally, the alteration—that results from the end of what is outrageously called "paganism" and the onset of Christianity, a change that runs so thoroughly deep that even an atheist as resolute as Hume cannot resist it.

However, in an earlier passage, an anachronistic and derogatory reference to the power of women opens out into a salient dimension that is present but concealed in Hume's text when given an alternate interpretation:

> In many nations, the female sex are reduced to like slavery, and are rendered incapable of all property, in opposition to their lordly masters. But though the males, when united, have in all countries bodily force sufficient to maintain this severe tyranny, yet such are the insinuation, address, and charms of their fair companions, that women are commonly able to break the confederacy, and share with the other sex in all the rights and privileges of society. (*EPM*, 191)

This cannot properly be read as included in the "power" component of Hume's notion of justice, which he presented in terms of physical qualities of strength and weakness entirely. Whatever his intentions, Hume's text here points to a state at least very much akin to Platonic *erōs*. This state is not the natural "conjunction" of the sexes, but rather an *atmosphere* that binds men and women. It is a reenactment of the birth of *Erōs* at the divine banquet where no wine was present, when Penia seduces Poros and gives birth in pure beauty to *Erōs*. In this reenactment, women begin to receive a measure of equality that will not only increase gradually, but that will come to liberate them from the need for marriage in order to secure property and their due place in society.

The myths, the playfulness, and in general the imagery so intrinsic to the Platonic dialogues find an appropriate counterpart in Hume's second *Enquiry*. They are as far as possible from being dispensable literary tropes or mere illustrations. Read rigorously—in yet another instance of Hume's text exceeding itself—justice is sited, and can only be sited, *in an image* and *as an image*. In terms of contemporary Continental philosophy, justice occurs *between*—between two images and their addenda, one glimpsed in *logos* through what is as close as possible to pure light and the other in the same way through pure darkness. The "secret springs" of justice—if such a phrase has any meaning at all—are just as resolutely closed off to us as are those of the ultimate causes of the "causes" that we discern (such as they are).

Part I cannot be called a *pan*egyric to justice—at least not in the unconditional sense used in connection with benevolence—since justice displays a darker side that is absent in the "softer" virtues as well as its happier side. However, Part I proceeds to its end in a positive manner and with several noteworthy remarks. The first, echoing the first city in speech in *Republic* II, locates justice in the need we have for one another in order to function as human beings. Another concerns the evolution of what we might call justice-consciousness:

> History, experience, reason sufficiently instruct us in this *natural* progress [from family, through individual society, to relations between societies] and in the gradual enlargement of our regards to justice, in proportion as we become acquainted with the extensive utility of that virtue. (*EPM*, 192; emphasis mine)

One cannot but wonder about a tension in Hume's text here. Against the "natural" educational process that familiarizes us with the utility of justice, he remarks—at least in effect, at least by extending his view of the "rational but much weaker beings"—that the more powerful social units may treat the less powerful in any manner that they wish, and with moral impunity. As odious as this notion sounds to contemporary ears, it can be viewed as belonging to the evolutionary growth of justice in human beings.[8] The tension certainly provokes questions that may be casuistical in form but consequential in practice. Sweatshops, even those in which conditions are particularly adverse, offer comparatively advantageous employment in certain regions where abject poverty predominates. Should they be closed? Should their owners, who have easy recourse to relocation, etc., be punished or forced to improve conditions, especially where governments are in league with them? I recall a particularly chilling documentary that features an eleven-year-old Thai girl who had been rescued from her position as a prostitute in Bangkok and returned to the country village where her family lived. Was she happy to have been rescued? No. She wished to return to her former trade so as to make money for her otherwise destitute family.

My *Imagination in Kant's Critique of Practical Reason*[9] can be read as a defense of Kantian moral theory, although it also functions as an excavation of the role of imagination in a text where it seems to play little or no role. The evolution of the sentiment of justice plays no part for Kant, whose writings on the particulars of justice derive from the categorical imperative. The main results are major and awe-inspiring, such as the respect for all humanity, freedom of speech, and autonomy. Others cannot stand up to scrutiny according to contemporary values, such as the restriction of the vote to property holders, the absolute sovereignty of government, and his many racist statements.

However, I strongly urge that we think these so-called "derivations" in a radically different manner—once again, in terms of *image-play*. With full confidence, we can directly derive p from $p \, \& \, q$, or q from $([p \rightarrow q] \, \& \, p)$. With equal confidence, and with undying gratitude to Hume, we know that we cannot directly derive any instance from the "concept" of cause. Kant's *Critique of Pure Reason,* his monumental attempt to answer Hume, conceded this and developed an elaborate apparatus of indirection that remains both controversial and very much alive. Therein lies the often shocking "applications" by Kant and Hume of their profound philosophical insights. However, if these insights are seen as *ruling images* rather than as "principles" (in the Newtonian sense, which both Hume and Kant occasionally claim for themselves)—or as principles in an ancient Greek sense as *archai,* as self-effacing and withdrawn beginnings along the lines of the *chōra* in Plato's *Timaeus*—then the "derivations" are transformed into what I will call a *mutual shining.* In this way, the philosophical contributions endure, though they are clearly finite; and they shine upon our practices in a manner that accounts for our finite historicality in such a way that slowly—perhaps too slowly, many would say—its flaws are brought to the glare of daylight and gradually overcome.

Part II

Hume carries forth the theme of utility in the second part of the second section just as he did in the first. However, he employs a series of phrases that seem at least virtually synonymous in order to characterize it: "the good of mankind" (*EPM,* 192); "the convenience and necessities of mankind" (*EPM,* 195); "the safety of the people" (*EPM,* 196); "the interest and happiness of human society" (*EPM,* 198); "the well-being of mankind and existence of society" (*EPM,* 199). These "criteria" are praised for their societal and intersocietal benefits, and so differ from the "softer" virtues that are lauded for the rewards they bring as a result of individual qualities. I shall first state the contents of his premises and conclusions and work backward to the more provocative notions in this section:

> First argument (citing Hume's text, but reorganizing the statements into P–C form:
> (P1) The necessity of justice to the support of society is the *sole* foundation of that virtue.
> (P2) . . . since no moral excellence is more highly esteemed [than usefulness].
> (C1, which becomes P1a) We may conclude that this circumstance of usefulness has, in general, the strongest energy and the most entire command over our sentiments.
> (C2a) It must therefore be a source of a considerable part of the merit ascribed to humanity, benevolence [etc.].

> (C2b) [A]nd it is the *sole* source of the moral approbation paid to fidelity, justice, veracity, integrity, and those other estimable and useful qualities.
>
> Condensing: necessity of justice & the highest esteem in which justice is held → usefulness the strongest command over sentiments → usefulness at least part of the homage paid to benevolence, etc., & the *sole* source of the moral approbation paid to fidelity, justice.

The first and most relevant aspect of this extended argument concerns what it purports to prove and what it abstains from proving. It addresses only the *ascription* of moral praise and blame. Once again, moral theory for Hume takes place in the determinate indeterminacy of the region between the poetical and philosophical fictions, that is, in the "real fiction" or play of images to which we are bound. Accordingly, the moral qualities praised are not unconditionally real qualities—they are not "pure being." Justice, especially, casts shadows, as we have seen.

Secondly, a superficial survey of this argument, even extending the most charitable interpretation to it, must call its soundness into question. Let us grant the truth of P1 as established by its place between the two fictions. P2, however, is at least problematic. In the modern moral philosophy of Hume's tradition, *order* has its defenders such as Hobbes. Closer to home, though Hutcheson posited utility as a sixth moral sense, Hume's dear friend and close colleague Adam Smith denied the existence of such a sense, arguing instead that there are moral qualities having nothing to do with utility:

> How selfish so ever man may be supposed, there are evidently some principles in his nature, which interest him in the fortunes of others, and render their happiness necessary to him, though he derives nothing from it except the pleasure of seeing it. Of this kind is pity or compassion, the emotion which we feel for the misery of others, when we either see it, or are made to conceive it in a very lively manner.[10]

What is utility or usefulness? The question seems unnecessary. However, given the broadness—might one also say the vagueness, or the emptiness, or perhaps even the falsity?—of the "utility" premise suggests that an attempt at addressing the question would prove . . . useful. While this section cannot be mapped quite so clearly onto corresponding sections of the appropriate Platonic dialogues, it is nevertheless instructive to make the attempt. At the outset of

Republic II, we find Adam Smith's sense and Hume's sense conflated. Glaucon asks Socrates to give his view concerning which of three kinds of goods justice belongs: (1) to those that we delight in for its own sake; (2) to those that we delight in both for its own sake and for the benefits they bring; and (3) to those that involve drudgery, and we engage in them only for the benefits they bring. To Socrates, justice belongs to the finest—*kallistō,* or most beautiful—kind, "the kind that a blessed man must like *(eudokimēseōn)* both for itself and for what comes out of it" (358a). If we translate "utility" back into Greek as a good *dia ta gignomena* (that comes into being from [justice]), then we see a nuanced distinction between ancient and modern "goodness." With "justice" at issue in the *Republic,* a brief aside into its most ancient senses may provide a reward.

Dikē (Justice) was one of the three Graces *(Hōrai).* Together with her sisters *Eunomia* (Good Order, Good Pasture) and *Eirēnē* (Peace, Spring), they secured good results for farmers by lawfully regulating the seasons and providing favorable soil conditions for crops. They evolved into genial guardians of cities, which required analogous ordering. *Dikē* was regarded as the secure foundation of cities as well as its moral center. Further, in passages Hume might have cited, she also exceeds all others in the approbation she receives, even from the gods:

> And there is virgin Justice, the daughter of Zeus, who is honored and reverenced among the gods who dwell on Olympus, and whenever anyone hurts her with lying slander, she sits beside her father, Zeus the son of Cronos, and tells him of men's wicked heart, until the people pay for the mad folly of their princes who, evilly minded, pervert judgment and give sentence crookedly.[11]

However, she departs the earth in disgust after the evil generation subsequent to the Golden Age unfolded into still greater depravity. Turning to the men of the Silver Age, *Dikē* curses them:

> Behold what manner of race the fathers of the Golden Age left behind them! Far meaner than themselves! But you will breed a viler progeny! Verily wars and cruel bloodshed shall be unto men and grievous woe shall be laid upon them.[12]

With *Dikē* having departed, *dikē* divested of its divine status becomes open to question in the *Republic,* where it is or seems to be defined politically as each of the three classes minding its own business, and is or seems to be defined psychically as each of the three parts of the soul minding *its* own business.[13] For Aristotle, justice is a moral virtue, a mean between two extremes. He offers no clear definition of justice, but divides it into distributive and rectificatory; for each, justice implies components of law-abidingness and fairness.

Hume's argument may suffer from a weak P2. However, his esteem for justice has an echo even more ancient than Plato or Aristotle, more ancient indeed than the discovery of logic. There can be no doubt concerning the quality, the power, the subtlety, the far-reaching consequences, and the continuing interest of Hume's argumentation. However, I would like to place his claim for the second *Enquiry* as being "of all my writings, historical, or literary, incomparably the best"[14] in a radical and perhaps transgressive context, a context that Hume would almost surely have found unacceptable. "[The second *Enquiry*] came unnoticed and unobserved into the world"[15] because the source from which it draws is *archaic*.

Hume's initial appeal is to a peculiar sense of *touch,* namely the touch of the *images* of right and wrong upon even the iciest sensibility. I suggest that this *touch* has significance beyond what we today often carelessly call "metaphoric." Rather, it points to a way of apprehension that is anterior to the sensible/intelligible distinction, and thus surely to the impressions/ideas and matter of fact/relation of ideas twofold that constitutes the field of knowledge as presented in the first *Enquiry*. Thus, the apparent paradox of Hume's supposed skepticism in theoretical matters but assurance in moral matters is resolved: Hume addresses theoretical matters critically but in terms of the kinds of dualism belonging to modern philosophy, but in the text of his practical philosophy archaic echoes are heard.

Of Political Society

This short and surprising section involves another modern reenactment of a Platonic—also an Aristophanic—trope. Its beginning follows its predecessor more or less unproblematically by extending the discourse on utility to relations between nations, where the bond it imposes is weaker:

> The observance of justice, though useful among them, is not guarded by so strong a necessity as among individuals; and the *moral obligation* holds proportion with the *usefulness*. All politicians will allow, and most philosophers, that reasons of state may, in particular emergencies, dispense with the rules of justice, and invalidate any treaty or alliance, where the strict observance of it

would be prejudicial, in a considerable degree, to either of the contracting parties. (*EPM*, 206)

However, a good deal of the remainder of the section concerns itself with the role of marriage in society, and the role of utility in sustaining the fundamentals of marriage. Or rather, it requires *one* fundamental, "the virtue of chastity or fidelity to the marriage bed" (*EPM*, 207). Once again, we feel the Greek spirit at odds with the Christianity-tainted atheist. In his consistently awkward way, Hume cites a passage from Plato's *Republic* V concerning the community of women in order to fit Plato into his position with regard to utility as the underlying support for the institution of marriage.[16] Without its utility (and without the apparently ancillary requirement of the "subsistence" of the married couple's children), "it will readily be owned, that such a virtue would never have been thought of" (*EPM*, 207).

A difference in degree, however, obtains between men and women regarding this "virtue." A man who offends against this virtue has surely committed a wrong. A woman who offends against it has violated an absolute proscription. Marital chastity of women guarantees the paternity of children and hence their identities and rights of property. The requirement of chastity for women is lifelong, well past childbearing age, for fear that the example set by a sexually active old women would exercise a pernicious influence on their younger cohort. Again, were it not for the usefulness of chastity, there would be no reason for it; indeed, the thought of it would never occur.

In the Platonic city in speech and in its Aristophanic counterpart, chastity played no role. As a historical note, Hippocrates recommended sexual activity for women since such activity promoted health. Abstinence is also absent from the behavior of most of the Olympian gods; The Platonic city featured manipulated marriages among members of the highest class—however, even when the greatest care would be taken to avoid the marriage of close relatives, incest was inevitable. Indeed, Socrates invokes the brother-sister "sacred marriage" of Zeus and Hera as the paradigm for human marriages. Further, after childbearing age, men and women were permitted to seek sexual satisfaction in any manner they wished. This comedy of the city[17] constituted one way of the attempted subjection of *erōs* to human law.

Aristophanes' comedy *Ecclēsiazousai (Assemblywomen)* presents another way, namely the enactment of a law whereby an equal measure of sexual satisfaction is guaranteed to all, just as equality governs every aspect of life in heroine Praxagora's Athens. Every woman is required to respond affirmatively to the entreaty of every man and vice versa—however, a young man must first satisfy an old woman before approaching a young woman, and a young woman must likewise satisfy an old man before enjoying the embraces of a young man. While the Platonic comedy abstracted primarily from the impossibility of avoiding incest, the Aristophanic comedy abstracts primarily from the impossibility of regulating human desire. In both comedies, *erōs* defeats all efforts—even those made only in speech—to bring it under human law.

In the *Symposium,* Socrates' recollected speech of Diotima presents a ladder of *erōs,* beginning from the love of one body and ascending to *erōs* of pure, utterly disembodied beauty. However, this final rung on the ladder is imaged only *conditionally*—she tells Socrates that "if" *(ei)* he could behold such beauty he would despise the bodily matters, and if *(ei)* human beings had the eyes to see such divine beauty they would bring forth beings rather than images. However, the raucous entry of drunken, disruptive, and beautiful-of-body Alcibiades—who is, perhaps peculiarly, welcome—upends this glorious encomium to ideal beauty and the *erōs* that would be drawn toward it if only it were possible. Within the *Symposium,* the Diotima-speech may be considered the Apollinian side of *erōs* and the arrival of Alcibiades, who proceeds to drown the meeting in wine, the Dionysian side.

Perhaps surprisingly, one can find echoes of this playful sex-comedic Greek spirit in Hume's retrograde view of "chastity or fidelity to the marriage bed." First of all, Hume concedes that if there were no use for it, the practice of chastity would never have been conceived. Sexual desire in men finds fewer constraints only because of its lesser social utility. If we were to turn our view away from the judgment of *prima facie* unfairness that we would impose upon Hume's double standard, we may discern the presence of a slowly emerging and evolving "city in speech" that turns out to be more insurrectionary than any occurring in their ancient analogues, with Praxagora's Athens excepted.

That women are denied the same satisfaction of their sexuality that men enjoy is indeed *prima facie* unfair. But the *individual* utility of this quality gradually results in massive social benefit. Perhaps I read too much into Hume when I ascribe the "insinuations, address, and charms" of women to their provocation in man of the ascent toward disembodied *erōs* rather than, for instance, to their sublimated sexual desire. Perhaps mine is a rereading informed by standards and concerns alien by nature to Hume's thought. However, the text implies that "all the rights and privileges of society" are *properly* theirs, and that Platonic disembodied *erōs* is the vehicle whereby this propriety first becomes possible. As indicated earlier, *de facto* progress toward full equality remains ongoing and cannot be found at all in certain countries on the earth. Nevertheless, nothing less than a transcendental signifier of some kind is required whereby men and women can determine their social and individual identity.

In a paper titled "Hume on the Gentler Sex," its author Jane Duran displays a keenly intuitive—and generous—philosophical impulse when she writes:

> I found that in beginning work on Hume's comments on women it became obvious that there is a nascent feminism in the work of this eighteenth century British thinker. I found—as I hoped—that Hume is fair, tolerant, and I think farsighted in his beliefs about relations between the sexes.[18]

Our views diverge, however, in the interpretation of erotic love (and of Plato on this subject, but that is another matter). She confines her attention to relations between the sexes alone, and situates the primary passion in bodily lust, with good will regarded as an ancillary passion. Chastity is required of women in order to guarantee paternity and so secure the responsibilities attaching to it for men.

A further difference is her exclusive concentration on the *Treatise,* where she astutely locates Hume's "nascent feminism" in his declaration that the opprobrium attaching to a woman's breach of chastity exceeds the *injustice* of her transgression—and, she reasons, therefore prepares the way for considerations of justice for women that will take place in the nineteenth century. She would, however, reject what I have called "a transcendental signifier," a position among feminists that is not uncommon. I am not certain that she has made her case that *Hume* "is fair, tolerant, and I think farsighted in his beliefs," but she has pointed to a way that the *text* of the *Treatise* can be opened out in this direction.

Annette C. Baier, in "Good Men's Women: Hume on Chastity and Trust," astutely notes:

> Males then have an obligation to be as chaste as women, but are, like princes, more readily *forgiven*, excused for lapses. This accords badly with Hume's proper evaluation of the importance of friendship in marriage, and its incompatibility with male sovereignty. That "entire and total union" which he takes as the *telos* of marriage would seem to be possible only if whatever restrictions there are on sexual freedom are mutual.[19]

However, she credits Hume with "recognition of the hard core of sexism."[20] Given the crude misogyny that Hume has expressed elsewhere and that I cited earlier, the dispassion of these scholars is commendable.

The more general outcome of which the above is a principal application is the natural need for *rules* in every social interaction, even the most troubling. One could say that while the establishment of rules is relative to many factors, it is a principle of morality—deriving from the *initial images of right and wrong* that dwell in every human breast—that there must be rules in every human social endeavor. This is the case between nations, within nations, in associations, and among thieves.

Why Utility Pleases

Part I

In this, the longest section of the second *Enquiry,* Hume resumes the pattern of devoting the first part primarily to praise of the utility/pleasure connection and the second part more to arguments concerning it. However, this section stands out by positing what I would call an explicitly *aesthetic* approach to moral philosophy. Like the preceding sections, its insights "derive"—if that is the most appropriate word—from the universally distributed images of right and wrong. Most strikingly, as will be shown, language—at least moral language—is bound to the nature of imagery. That is to say, it is *not* fundamentally conceptual; the fundament is the aforementioned natural imagistic bond:

> Had nature made no such distinction, founded on the original constitution of the mind, the words, *honourable* and *shameful, lovely* and *odious, noble* and *despicable,* had never had place in any language; nor could politicians, had they invented these terms, ever have been able to render them intelligible, or make them convey any idea to the audience. So that nothing can be more superficial than this paradox of the skeptics. . . .
>
> The social virtues must, therefore, be allowed to have a natural beauty and amiableness, which at first, antecedent to all precept or education, recommends them to the esteem of uninstructed mankind, and engages their affections. (*EPM,* 214)

Crucially, anteriority belongs to the *images* of right and wrong. The more philosophically habitual original/image relation is either reversed or effaced altogether. We discern the qualities conformable to the anterior images *subsequently,* just as we interpret the language that names them, that is to say, describes them.

Since utility is the major source of the merit of these positive qualities, Hume concludes that the end that these qualities tend to promote "must be some way agreeable to us, and take hold of some natural affection" (*EPM*, 214). Thus: images of right and wrong → ability to discern "amiable" qualities → natural beauty of amiable qualities → utility of amiable qualities → utility (toward its end) partakes in some way of their natural beauty → utility pleases in some way. In what way? In its *unselfish* self-showing. Against the view that morals are reducible to self-love—a position regarding justice held by Aristotle and even by Polybius, whom Hume respected highly, Hume appeals to the same images of right and wrong in the human breast to demonstrate the untenability of this view.

Imagine a noble deed performed in distant times that has no direct effect upon us or anything in our current situation, for example, Socrates offering the receipt of free lunches in lieu of his death sentence, or Thomas More's refusal on principle to swear to the oath upon the Act of Succession. We admire such acts immediately, however distant and however alien to our own circumstances. Similarly, such acts performed by our proximate enemies also draw praise even though they work against our interests. As a lifelong Democrat and as a despiser of the conduct of the administration of George W. Bush, his selection of two African Americans to serve in major cabinet positions remains admirable in my eyes.

For the first time, an African American (Colin Powell)—though one with whom I disagreed strongly—could order young Americans of all races to go into harm's way; and though many of her decisions seemed dreadful to me, African American Condoleezza Rice rose above the level of her peers in her service as our diplomatic leader. Just as easily, a strict and harsh conservative such as Charles Krauthammer ascribes a "first rate mind" to Barack Obama, whose every policy he both opposes and deems dangerous.

If morals were grounded in accord with what Hume calls "the selfish principle," our hearts could not take pleasure from actions (a) in which we have no interest or (b) that work against our interest. Utility can therefore not possibly mean merely "utility for me," but extends way farther by the nature of the human heart. In Part II, Hume proposes to "open up" this general principle and to demonstrate why it supplies "one great source of moral distinctions" (*EPM*, 218).

Part II

Utility therefore extends to others as well as to myself, and aims at increasing what Hume calls "the happiness of mankind." He cites Bacon's *experimentum crucis*, which had been already undertaken in Part I, "which points out the right way in any doubt or ambiguity" (*EPM*, 219). What guarantees the "rightness" of his account of the immediate pleasure evoked by utility that is aimed at the happiness of mankind? Once again, it is the unity of the human heart:

> In general, it is certain, that, wherever we go, whatever we reflect on or converse about, everything still presents us with the view of human happiness or misery, and excites in our breast a sympathetic movement of pleasure or uneasiness. In our serious occupations, in our careless amusements, this principle still exerts its active energy. (*EPM*, 221)

Sympathy, *sym-pathein*, means undergoing together, undergoing together-with.

Although his intended aim almost certainly differs from my interpretation, his text most surely supports it. Hume's most intriguing proof (*apodeixis!*) is what must be called not merely the play of images, but the *magical* play of images:

> Every movement of the theatre, by a skilful poet, is communicated, as it were by magic, to the spectators; who weep, tremble, resent, rejoice, and are inflamed with all the variety of passions, which actuate the several personages of the drama. (*EPM*, 221–22)

In terms of the Aristotelian view of poetry, which Hume largely shares, plays are imitations of actions first of all. Everyone involved, from the poet, through the director, the actors, the various designers, and the spectators, knows that the performance does not belong to everyday life. So the qualifier "as it were" indicates that by "magic" Hume merely points metaphorically to a paradox in which real passion emerges from a process that is knowingly fictitious in principle all the way down.

However, the somewhat more ancient but inestimably more radical Platonic account of the effect of poetry in the *Ion* seems more suitable to Hume's account here. In the *Ion*, the stone of Heraclea plays the role of Hume's "as it were, magic," and pulls every element of the dramatic experience together. If we were to enumerate the differences between the two accounts for convenience, we would say that the Platonic account adds two members at the head, although these are of a different order than the rest: the god → the Muse → the poet → the rhapsode (here, the actor would serve as analogue) → the spectators. However, a dynamism from another dimension shows that this enumeration is a superficial one: the divine madness of the poet, whose ordinariness in his sober state is a stark contrast to it:

> For a poet is an airy thing, winged and holy, and he is not able to make poetry until he becomes inspired and out of his mind and his intellect is no longer in him. As long as a human being has his intellect in his possession he will always lack the power to make poetry or sing prophesy. (534b–c)

In light of his painstaking distinction of the passions from the understanding, and in light of his insistence that moral principles are primarily matters of sentiment, Hume's implicit poetics inclines toward a nonrational view of the origin of poetry and of its reception. Thus, his "skilful poet" seems to be at odds with his nonrational—or only secondarily rational—poetics. Surely, the Homer of whom Socrates speaks writes melodically, rhythmically, and metrically. Homer's madness, and the madness of those drawn into the performance of his poetry, does not exclude measure at all; rather, this divine madness displays it to the highest degree. Here is yet another instance of Hume's text working against itself and in so doing, disclosing an archaic, "magical," origin anterior to the traditional mimesis and Hume's modern division of understanding and passion.

The ongoing reversal of the image/original relation occurs once again in Hume's statement of the function of poetry:

> It is the business of poetry to bring every affection near to us by lively imagery and representation, and make it look like truth and reality: A certain proof, that, wherever that reality is found, our minds are disposed to be strongly affected by it. (*EPM*, 222–23)

Read rigorously, poetry shapes its images in accord with the universal images of right and wrong in the human heart; from this it derives its power to move its spectators, and from this it performs its service as the "premise" for the proof of instances of this image-play that are found in "reality." In Hume's moral philosophy, "reality" has second-order status.

So what occurs, then, in every apprehension of moral actions, including one's own? *Some* pleasure is taken in actions useful for the good of humanity, even when these actions are at odds with our immediate interests and when they are remote from our present concerns. Hume's explanation, however, takes a more or less unusual turn:

> And if the principles of humanity are capable, in many instances, of influencing our actions, they must, at all times, have *some* authority over our sentiments, and give us a general approbation of what is useful to society, and blame of what is dangerous or pernicious. The

degrees of these sentiments may be the subject of controversy; but the reality of their existence, one should think, must be admitted in every theory or system. (*EPM,* 226)

Although this argument seems both sound and sufficiently modest in its conclusion, one must ask: The principles of humanity—are they not *sentiments* themselves? Surely they derive from an original sentiment, the image of right and wrong that dwells in every human breast. I would call the principles of humanity *ruling sentiments* or *images,* sentiments that provide the measure for the more specific sentiments to which we are given over.

The recognition of this "epistemological" determination is necessary in order to account for the differences in degree of certain sentiments, and in certain situations, and for different moral evaluations and practices of different spectators and actors. It justifies the claim that no one is entirely indifferent to the softer virtues. It also answers the implicit question of the section's title "Why Utility Pleases." As a natural pleasure obtains when the happiness of humankind is advanced, and as utility is the quality by which the happiness of humankind is advanced, it follows that utility pleases—and does so immediately. This pure pleasure, of course, is often mixed with pain occasioned by blameworthy qualities or by sympathy at the plight of unjust treatment toward others. However, this purity echoes—at least to some degree and in significant analogy with—the disembodied *erōs* spoken of in Plato's *Symposium* and the selfless *erōs* spoken of in his *Phaedrus.*

Prelude to sections VI, VII, and VIII

The transition to these three sections reminds of the redirection of the discourse of *Republic* II. While the matter at the center of the *Republic* appears more specific—namely, the nature of justice and not of morality generally—the commonalities are conspicuous enough to require attention.

First of all, Socrates believes that he has already shown the superiority of justice to injustice in Book I. With Glaucon and Adeimantus demanding that he show them both its intrinsic value and the benefits it brings to the just man, Socrates professes his inadequacy since "when I thought I showed in what I said to Thrasymachus that justice is better than injustice, you didn't accept it from me" (368b). Toward persuading the two interlocutors, he proposes his famous alternative:

I'll tell you, I said. There is, we say, justice of one man; and there is, surely, justice of a whole city, too?

> Certainly, he said.
> Is a city bigger than one man?
> Yes, it is bigger, he said.
> [I]f you want, first we'll investigate what justice is like in the cities. Then we'll go on to consider it in individuals, considering the likeness of the bigger in the *idea* of the littler. (368e–369a)

Hume does not trumpet this translocation from "bigger" to "littler" in his move from attention to humankind writ large to individual human beings. Nevertheless, he ascribes a similarly strong analogical relation in which the larger, moral realm serves to illuminate the "smaller" realm of human qualities:

> Now this distinction [between what is useful and what is pernicious] is the same in all its parts, with the *moral distinction,* whose foundation has been so often, and so much in vain, enquired after. The same endowments of the mind, in every circumstance, are agreeable to the sentiment of morals and to that of humanity; . . . By all the rules of philosophy, therefore, we may conclude, that these sentiments are originally the same; since, in each particular, even the most minute, they are governed by the same laws, and are moved by the same objects. (*EPM,* 235–36)

Like the Platonic analogy, Hume's analogy breaks down at a crucial point. But as we will see, it does so in such a way as to disclose major insights about moral life.

Section VI: Of Qualities Useful to Ourselves; Section VII: Of Qualities Immediately Agreeable to Ourselves; Section VIII: Of Qualities Immediately Agreeable to Others

Part I

I suggest that the three catalogues of qualities be looked at first of all as *purifications,* that is, as attempts to avoid (1) encroachment of the agreeable (the loved) upon the useful (the beneficial) generally; (2) the encroachment of the agreeable upon the useful with respect to oneself; and (3) the encroachment of the useful altogether upon what others love in us. Within each of the three sections, a twist occurs toward its end that complicates these purifications; also, insofar as the third section concerns *immediate* agreeableness, we may expect some measure of discontinuity with its predecessors.

Concerning qualities useful to ourselves, Hume begins by asserting that no quality is absolutely praise or blameworthy but requires "a due medium" (*EPM*, 233). To this idea, first championed by the Peripatetics, Hume adds: "But this medium is chiefly determined by utility" (*EPM*, 233). In Part I, he offers images of certain qualities from history in order to secure this view, which he regards as *almost* self-evident. These are presented as qualities directed toward a certain end, a more limited end than the happiness of humankind. One wonders, in light of this, whether they are properly called moral qualities, or whether for Hume a split occurs in the notion of morals, namely a split between *right* on one hand and *prudential* on the other.

In this light, I shall consider *discretion*, which occurs differently and is regarded differently in different circumstances. To Cromwell and Cardinal de Retz, "discretion may appear an alderman-like virtue, as Dr. Swift calls it" (*EPM*, 236), by virtue of their penchant for stirring up (and, in the case of the former, engaging in) military conflict to realize their great ambition. However, this virtue has the greatest usefulness in ordinary life, as it both furthers the aim of success and prevents all manner of failures and disappointments. For Hume, it constitutes the necessary quality for the conduct of an effective life, for even if an individual has the panoply of other useful qualities they will be of little avail if discretion is lacking. Hume's analogue is the powerful Polyphemus, whose superiority in strength and whose independence cannot save him from the machinations of Odysseus, although he has Odysseus and his men trapped in his lair.

The quality of discretion may, of course, be employed in a most blameworthy manner. Hume writes: "He is happy, whose circumstances suit his temper; but he is more excellent, who can suit his temper to any circumstances" (*EPM*, 237). However, this adage clearly serves the astute criminal no less than it serves the human being who seeks to live rightly. Moral qualities are marked by their usefulness, but this proposition is hardly convertible. Discretion is a useful quality without being a moral quality. So too are industry and frugality, when they are practiced in due measure. They are, therefore, necessary but not sufficient conditions for a moral life, that is, a life that consists of *some* contribution to the happiness of humankind.

However, some qualities partake of both prudence and rightness, although they too are necessary but not sufficient:

> *Honesty, fidelity, truth,* are praised for their immediate tendency to promote the interests of society; but after those virtues are once established upon this foundation, they are also considered as ad-

vantageous to the person himself, and as the source of that trust
and confidence, which alone can give a man any consideration in
life. One becomes contemptible . . . when he forgets the duty,
which . . . he owes to himself as well as to society. (*EPM*, 238)

The parallel Hume makes between social utility and utility to individuals echoes the parallel between Socrates' parallel between the big letters and the little letters concerning the pursuit of justice. However, just as in the case of the latter, the parallel is disrupted in Part II of this section.

Part II

As indicated earlier, just as the Greek *aretē* has undertones of power or notable skill in addition to moral excellence, for Hume *morals* have undertones of power or notable skill in addition to moral rightness. These undertones sound with particular resonance here, where Hume writes:

It may not be improper . . . to examine the influence of bodily
endowments, and of the goods of fortune, over our sentiments
of regard and esteem, and to consider whether these phenomena
fortify or weaken the present theory. (*EPM*, 244)

Like the qualities of mind, the utility of these qualities varies with various situations. A beautiful and/or a strong body in ancient times, when technology was considerably less advanced, was less useful in Hume's day than in ancient Greece and Rome, just as it is less useful in our day than in Hume's. Nevertheless, beauty and/or strength surely have *some* measure of utility, both to the happiness of society and to the person endowed with one or both of these traits. Further, they are generally admired—in, for example, many celebrities and athletes.

The possession of riches, whether as a gift of fortune or as the result of industry, also has a measure of utility both for the society and for the individual. Although Hume does not expressly say so, this possession—like the quality of discretion—can serve as a means to harmfulness. Hume notes the conflict that frequently occurs in the regard paid to it: while riches are admired for the associated images of prosperity, comfort, etc., this admiration often gives way to jealousy, to a much greater degree than the admiration given to beauty or strength. And finally, in a manner that can most appropriately be called Socratic, the admiration for both gifts of fortune and admiration for riches gives way to another measure entirely:

> A man who has cured himself of all ridiculous prepossessions, and is fully, sincerely, and steadily convinced, from experience as well as philosophy, that the difference of fortune makes less difference in happiness than is vulgarly imagined; such a one does not measure out degrees of esteem according to the rent-rolls of his acquaintance. [While he might show greater outward deference to the lord than to the vassal], his internal sentiments are more regulated by the personal characters of men, than by the accidental and capricious favours of fortune. (*EPM,* 248)

In this twenty-first century, the "lord" does not receive the kind of automatic deference to which Hume refers in this passage. However, the now-healthy human being judges according to the same "internal sentiments." Thus, while different circumstances yield different practices in accord with the different measures of utility, the result of "experience as well as philosophy" discloses *personal character* as both most useful to the person and most esteemed in others. The attainment of this perspective requires a cure—*purification*—from the variable judgments of utility.

Socrates says in the *Gorgias,* "For I say that the admirable and good person *(kalon kai agathon)* is happy *(eudaimona),* while the one who is unjust and wicked is miserable *(athlion)*" (470e). Deservedly respected Hume scholar Annette Baier suggests that Hume has no answer (and realizes that he has no answer) to the one she calls the accomplished or clever knave, who succeeds in his evil designs and remains closed off totally from the principles of morals. However, it is worth reminding that *eudaimonia* as implying health with respect to one's spirit is hardly synonymous with happiness as the unreflective fulfillment of individual desires. Its counterpart *athlios* implies a like wretchedness and misery of spirit that cuts far more deeply than mere distress over one's designs being thwarted.

What can be said, then, to the supposed counterexample of the "clever knave"? I would maintain that the clever knave is no counterexample, but rather marks the limit of that for which any moral philosophy can account. The moral realm is defined by the images of right and wrong that dwell in every human breast. If a person either lacks such images or, what is far more likely, has such images but regards them as weaknesses in both himself and in others—somehow useless and/or disagreeable—then he does not regard himself, nor is he, a member of the moral realm. If his cleverness should ever fail him, he is a most unlikely prospect for rehabilitation.

Section VII: Of Qualities Immediately Agreeable to Ourselves

Not until the end of this section do we discover its systematic purpose: both the qualities useful to oneself and those that are immediately agreeable to oneself derive from the one common source, namely *sympathy*. And as has already been shown, sympathy—also called "fellow-feeling" from time to time—derives from the shared moral imagery that inhabits the human breast. When this moral imagery directs toward the softer sentiments, they disclose their penchant toward the good of humanity. When it directs toward the somewhat sterner virtue of justice, the latter discloses its social utility as promoting the happiness of humankind, although this happiness does not obtain in every particular case. When it directs toward political society, the enactment of utility is more varied and less permanent than in the case of justice due to the shifting interests of states.

Because utility advances the aims of both societies and individuals, it "is a source of praise and approbation" (*EPM*, 231), that is, it is loved because the human heart beats along with it. So too, in a special way, does a personal character that has purified itself from externals that call its shine into question. To ascribe intrinsic value to such a character means no more and no less than such a person's bearing and actions harmonize with the image of rightness as they repel the image of wrong. This chapter introduces something new and delicate to the image-play of the second *Enquiry*, namely, a kind of self-regard that can be clearly distinguishable from what Hume earlier called self-love.

Hume's rough catalogue of such qualities here draw from literature and history more than in any other section. This strategy has two salutary results: it focuses on the *qualities* that we come to love in ourselves rather than ourselves *simpliciter*, and it presents vicarious images of these qualities rather than definitions. Some qualities, such as cheerfulness, require no such treatment because it is clear that cheerfulness makes those who have this quality . . . cheerful! A part of this agreeability stems from the way it spreads to others—contra Horace, who maintains that "the melancholy hate the merry" (*EPM*, 250). By contrast, the character of Cassius who, in the words of Caesar, eschewed and despised smiles, neither takes enjoyment in himself nor in others and so represents a kind of danger.

Magnanimity or greatness of mind (*megalopsychia* in Greek), on the other hand, can make itself manifest in many ways. So Hume—drawing on Longinus's *On the Sublime*, which maintains that the sublime is often nothing but the image of magnanimity—provides many different images. Their difference accords with the variable situations in which it is found. His first is the image of Ajax in *Odyssey* XI, who responds to the impassioned entreaty of Odysseus to stay his anger at the gift of the armor with a silence "which expresses more noble disdain and resolute indignation than any language can convey" (*EPM*, 252). When the lesser Parmenio tells Alexander that he, Parmenio, would accept Darius's offer if he were Alexander, the latter replies that he, too, would accept Darius's offer—if he were Parmenio. Medea, when asked what support she has against her many enemies, replies "*Myself I say, and it is enough*" (*EPM*, 253).

Although the quality of *courage* is clearly useful both to society and to the individual, Hume notes that "this quality has a peculiar lustre, which it derives wholly from itself" (*EPM*, 254). In order to demonstrate this luster in vicarious imagery, Hume turns first to Demosthenes' account of King Philip II of Macedon, whom Demosthenes despised for his tyrannical ambition and to whom he urged his fellow Athenians in memorable speeches not to surrender under any circumstances. However:

> "I beheld Philip . . . he with whom was your contest, resolutely, while in pursuit of empire and dominion, exposing himself to every wound; his eye gored, his neck wrested, his arm, his thigh pierced, whatever part of his body fortune should seize on, that cheerfully relinquishing; provided that, with what remained, he might live in honour and renown . . ." (*EPM*, 254)

Nevertheless, Demosthenes' praise of Philip's courage can be considered and loved apart from the rest of what the encomiast of his courage regarded as his otherwise contemptible character.

The Romans, as a predominantly military society, went so far as to equate courage with virtue itself. Herodotus reported that the Scythians used the scalps of their victims as towels, and whoever acquired the most such towels was most esteemed and—we may presume—had the greatest self-esteem:

> So much had martial bravery, in that nation, as well as in many others, destroyed the sentiments of humanity; a virtue surely much more useful and engaging. It is indeed observable, that, among all uncultivated nations, who have not, as yet, had full experience of the advantages attending beneficence, justice, and the social virtues, courage is the predominant excellence; what is most celebrated by poets, recommended by parents and instructors, and admired by the public in general. The ethics of Homer are, in this particular, very different from those of Fénelon, his elegant imitator . . . (*EPM*, 255)[21]

In "Of the Standard of Taste," which shall be treated in the following chapter, Hume claims that both he and Fénelon "inculcate the same moral precepts, and . . . bestow their applause and blame on the same virtues and vices" (*OST,* 134–35). By "ethics" here, Hume refers to manners and conduct; however, much of this concurrence can be attributed to the nature of language, in which the word for virtue in any tongue implies praise and vice implies blame. He thus reads Homer astutely even as he notes that Achilles and Ulysses conduct themselves otherwise than does Telemachus in Fénelon's epic:

> HOMER'S general precepts, where he delivers any such, will never be controverted; but it is obvious, that, when he draws particular pictures of manners, and represents heroism in <u>ACHILLES</u>, and prudence in <u>ULYSSES</u>, he intermixes a much greater degree of ferocity in the former, and of cunning and fraud in the latter, than FENELON would admit of. The sage ULYSSES, in the GREEK poet, seems to delight in lies and fictions, and often employs them without any necessity, or even advantage. But his more scrupulous son, in the FRENCH epic writer, exposes himself to the most imminent perils, rather than depart from the most exact line of truth and veracity. (*OST,* 135)

Megalopsychia belongs to all three poetic heroes alike. However, the question arises: In what way does this quality derive from the original moral imagery, just as benevolence and humanity do? There certainly seems to be an overlay of *power* in the notion of heroic virtue. However, this overlay may be set aside in the act of interpretation.

The same question can be raised in connection with "that undisturbed philosophical tranquility, superior to pain, sorrow, anxiety, and each assault of adverse fortune" (*EPM,* 256). Hume suggests that this tranquility is a form of magnanimity, and presents Socrates and Epictetus as paradigms of this virtue. However, in noting what he calls "our narrow souls" (*EPM,* 256), which would regard such strength of mind as excessive, he also comments that the ancient philosophical heroes would find "our" advances in the softer virtues, in justice, and in government excessive "had any one been able then to have made a fair representation of them" (*EPM,* 257). "Fair representation" can mean both "accurate" and "beautiful." The two are not mutually exclusive, However, I suggest that both the subject matter and the context incline strongly toward the latter.

Toward the end of Section VII, Hume perhaps surprisingly catalogues poetical charm among the qualities useful to the one who can deliver it by "a mechanism of nature, not easy to be explained" (*EPM*, 259). The gifted poet's fame endures, while that of the political achievers wanes. I do not doubt that the name Sarah Palin is more widely recognized today in America than that of James Madison. Hume honors the qualities of Augustus that enabled him to manage the Roman Empire such that unprecedented peace and liberty prevailed during his rule.[22] But this magnificent achievement, together with

> all the splendour of his noble birth and imperial crown, render[s] him but an unequal competitor for fame with Virgil, who lays nothing into the opposite scale but the divine beauties of his poetical genius. (*EPM*, 259–60)

The same holds for the fame enjoyed by poets at the expense of philosophers, despite the many gains they have made possible. However, the philosopher is the one who can provide due acclaim to the accomplishment of poets:

> [The listing of] the great charm of poetry consists in lively pictures of the sublime passions, magnanimity, courage, disdain of fortune; or those of the tender affections, love, and friendship; which warm the heart, and diffuse over it similar sentiments and emotions. (*EPM*, 259)

Of the untold millions who have practiced philosophy as a formal discipline and/or as a way of life, no more than a few names from its long history have even the slightest resonance with the public. Most unjustly, perhaps, the name of the incomparable David Hume is also obscure outside official philosophical circles.

In this light, Hume's extolment of poetry may seem especially ironic as well as opposed to the conventional Platonic view that poetry (which is essentially imitation) is third from truth, therefore falsifies, and so presents a great danger to the soul. I have argued an opposite view as forcefully and energetically as I can in many places, as have others that I have cited already. To indicate this view as briefly as I can for my purposes here, I shall look at *Republic* X, one of the apparently clearest sites of the conventional view. Socrates appears to mock the talent of the imitator, likening him to a person who carries a mirror everywhere:

> [Q]uickly you will make the sun and the things in the heaven; quickly, the earth; and quickly, yourself and the other animals and plants and everything else that was just now mentioned.

Yes, he said, so that they look like they *are;* however, they surely *are* not in truth.

Fine *(kalōs)* I said, and you engage the *logos* as is necessary.²³ (596e)

This "analysis" places not only the painters but far more importantly the tragic poets (with Homer as their leader) below the craftspeople in status, as the latter produce actual things (e.g., furniture) as they sight the *idea* of each thing while the imitators merely present reproductions of what nature and craft actually produce, while having no real knowledge of them. But consider Socrates' indictments of Homer: (1) no cities were better governed thanks to him; no war was well fought by virtue of his advice; (2) he handed down no way of life, as did the Pythagoreans, for example; (3) finally and most significantly of all, he did not educate human beings so as to lead them toward wisdom—as did Sophists such as Protagoras!

Every charge that Socrates levels against Homer can be leveled against himself. Further, Socrates blames Homer . . . for not being a Sophist! In addition, recall the Socratic claim in the *Ion* concerning the nonrational, divine inspirational source of poetry, which benefits humankind although knowledge plays no role in this benefit. Still further, recall the qualification in *Republic* III that poetry can harm the young . . . who are not aware that it may have an underlying sense *(huponoia)*. This underlying sense is tacitly endorsed on numerous occasions by Socrates, who frequently cites Homer approvingly. The most impressive example occurs in the *Republic,* where the following Homeric passage is cited in two entirely different contexts:

> I would rather be on the soil, a serf to another,
> To a man without lot whose means of life are not great,
> Than rule over all the dead who have perished.²⁴

In the context of the education of the guardians, who are trained to identify the good of the city and their own good, this is the first poetic phrase that is censored (386c). To show the great hero Achilles expressing dread at his death would only instill a most unwanted fear of death in the guardians-in-training. However, the same passage is the very first one directed toward the person who has been liberated from the cave and who has grown accustomed to life on earth. Having been liberated from the region of shadows/blind opinions without substance, and having accustomed himself to a life nearer the truth, the "Achilles in Hades" passage would resonate in a thoroughly different register. Socrates holds up the image of the man chained in the cave who receives prizes and honors for his ability to best predict the order of the shadows on the wall, and asks whether the liberated man would desire such honors:

> Or, rather, would he be affected as Homer says and want very much "to be on the soil, a serf to another man, and to a portionless man, and to undergo anything whatsoever rather than to opine those things and live that way." (516d)

Carrying the latter context into Hume's Section VII of the second *Enquiry*, the Homeric passage presents a sublime image, an image of that greatness of mind that despises any life other than one directed toward truth. Two outgrowths concerning the Hume/Plato relation emerge from this transposition. The first concerns the content of a life directed toward truth. Both Hume in the first *Enquiry* and Socrates throughout the dialogues fearlessly follow their questioning wherever it leads, and both conclude their questioning by affirming their ignorance of even the most fundamental matters. They share another quality useful to oneself, namely, a cheerfulness that otherwise might seem out of place in the one whose rigorous search resulted in so apparently dark a result.

The second, however, marks a difference between ancient Platonic and modern Humean poetics that sheds considerable light on each. In the Platonic dialogues, poetry involves divine inspiration and—as indicated by the two contexts of the "Achilles in Hades" passage—*interpretation (hermēneia)*. The question concerning taste does not arise, nor is the concept beauty isolated and studied abstractly. Hume speaks of poetry in terms of its lively presentation of the passions. Perhaps he echoes the Aristotelian view of poetry as imitation, but only in that most general way. He also holds that taste in the discerning perception of the work of great poets deserves its own special praise:

> The very sensibility to these beauties, or a *delicacy* of taste, is itself a beauty in any character; as conveying the purest, the most durable, and most innocent of all enjoyments. (*EPM*, 260; emphasis mine)

This extraordinary praise requires close attention, for it elevates delicacy of taste above *philosophy* not only as a quality that is useful to oneself, but as one that exceeds all others in significant and distinctive ways. The claim of its supreme purity places it above the conventional interpretation of Plato's so-called but nonexistent theory of Forms, according to which (in a decontextualized reading of parts of the *Republic*), the greatest pleasure derives from their contemplation. A more fitting dialogical comparison arises in connection with the *Philebus* where beauty is more explicitly thematized than in the *Republic*.

In the latter, Socrates says of the good that it is "beyond being, exceeding it in dignity and power" (509b). In the *Philebus*, the good finds itself both accessible in a way and protected from despoliation:

> SOCRATES: So now the power of the good has taken refuge in the nature of the beautiful; for measure and proportion are everywhere identified [*sumbainei*—"stand together with"] with beauty and virtue.
>
> PROTARCHUS: Certainly.
>
> SOCRATES: Then if we cannot catch the good with one idea, let us run it down with three—beauty, proportion, and truth, and let us say that these, considered as one, may more properly than all other components of the mixture be regarded as the cause, and that through the goodness of these the mixture has been made good. (64e–65a)

Admittedly, it is something of a stretch to read the Platonic account here into a Humean context. Socrates does not speak of poetry here, nor does Hume speak expressly of goodness or truth. I shall only mention my opinion, and not employ it in this analogy, that the question of beauty in relation to taste does not come up for Plato since the ancients of his time dwelled within beauty that was ever-present, too close to require such inquiry. Recalling Socrates' second speech in the *Phaedrus*, beauty alone among the *eidē* shines into the human realm and enables the recollection of the other *eidē*. For Hume, either one cannot speak of such shining at all, or—as I interpret his thought here—the shining confines itself to a very few special objects and requires a series of quite demanding conditions in order to gain access to it, as will be shown in the next chapter.

For Hume, delicacy in the perception of beauty is itself beautiful, a sentiment that also has a suggestive Platonic echo. In the *Symposium*, a dialogue recollected years after the eponymous event of a dinner honoring the young and victorious tragedian Agathon, Socrates is presented uncharacteristically, that is, dressed decoratively and with sandaled feet. When his companion Aristodemus inquires as to the reason for this unusual appearance, Socrates replies: "So that beauty might match beauty *(. . . hina kalos para kalon iō)*" (174a). While this cryptic answer invites several interpretations,[25] the one that seems most germane here has Socrates contesting the beauty of philosophy with the beauty of poetry. It is unclear which prevails in the contest. Both Agathon and Aristophanes fall into a drunken sleep as Socrates soon leaves and spends his day as usual. This seems to signal a victory for philosophy, although the dice may well be loaded since the dialogue is written by a philosopher. However, in Socrates' speech, he relates the words of his teacher Diotima with approval:

> Everyone would choose for himself to give birth to these sorts of children [i.e., children of the soul] rather than human ones. Men look at Homer and Hesiod and the other great poets and are jealous of the kind of offspring they left behind them, because they are the kind of beings which afford to those men a deathless fame and memory. Or, if you like, she went on, Lycurgus, the savior of Lacedaemonia. . . . And Solon . . . on account of his creation of the laws . . . (209d–e)

Poetry is given place ahead even of law-giving, a distant but distinguishable complement to Hume's claim that the beauties of poetry are the most lasting in addition to being the purest. His most interesting and—at least in relation to Plato—most controversial claim concerns the maximum *innocence* ascribed to the enjoyment of poetry. However Plato's view of poetry is interpreted, it cannot be described as an innocent pleasure, that is to say, as free of effect on the one who enjoys it. The notion of the *disinterested pleasure* attending works of art does not arise in any manner in the Platonic dialogues. The distance between knower and object known has not yet been opened in such a way as to allow for such a response. To say the same thing from the modern side, the duality between reason and sentiment operative in the second *Enquiry* cannot be found in Plato. Indeed, the Greek word commonly translated as intellect or reason (*nous*, the activity of which is *noēsis*) is listed under affections (*pathēmata*) or *passions* of the soul.

The best I can do to sustain this part of the parallel is to remind of Socrates' continued friendship toward Homer (595b), and of the obvious point that Homeric poetry has not harmed him. Another possible aspect of the parallel can be found in the employment of salient poetical phrases by both Hume and Plato at key moments of their discourse. However, these likenesses do not obviate the differences between the ancient and modern perspectives of each. These differences, however, receive their decisive markings in this comparison, as will be shown in the following chapter.

It appears that we have traveled far from the animating question awakened by Hume's text, namely how qualities agreeable to ourselves are "*of a kind* similar to that other sentiment, which arises from views of a public or private utility" (*EPM,* 260; emphasis mine). How, in other words, do such qualities as cheerfulness, strength of mind, tranquility, and delicacy arise from those images in the human heart of right and wrong from which the moral qualities derive? Could it be a kind of modern overlap of the ancient Greek overlap of *aretē* (virtue) as morality and as power? I cautiously suggest that this is so. Is it "wrong" to be gloomy, weak-willed, excitable, or crude? Surely not in the sense that these qualities are evil or, in gentler language, actively harmful to the happiness of humanity. But in a sense, they are: according to another of Hume's major criteria, no one would choose to have these traits ascribed to her or him. They indicate that some capacity is lacking that might otherwise be present.

The human heart, therefore, beats sympathetically with cheerfulness, strength of mind, tranquility, and delicacy as it recoils from their opposites.

Section VIII: Of Qualities Immediately Agreeable to Others

Hume again separates immediate agreeability from utility and, though he does not say so expressly, seems to assume that these qualities also derive from the same source in the human heart as the other useful and agreeable qualities. This list is, to my mind, rather less impressive: good manners, wit, conversational skill, modesty, eloquence (as refraining from self-praise), and that grace that escapes language but is both recognized everywhere and always pleases—a certain *je ne sais quoi*, as the cultivated are wont to say. Perhaps from the same ancient/modern asymmetry on the issue of poetry and/or perhaps from the lack of these qualities in my own bearing, I find this list the most arbitrary and time-bound of all. I cannot help but think of Socrates: Well-mannered? Witty (in Hume's sense)? Immediately agreeable to all others? Rhetorically skilled? Adept at smooth, easy conversation? Modest (recall his claim that the god sent him on a special mission, and that no Greek is wiser)? Gracefully charming?

As already noted, this text challenges the contemporary reader with its time-bound and (by our standards) repellent racism, sexism, and colonialism. However, these can be eliminated or at least substantially mitigated by employing Hume's own standards, especially his point of origin in the right/wrong imagery of the human heart. For the only occasion in this text, I am unable to save this section or any part of it. None of these traits can be deemed "right" except in the most superficial sense, that is, they are nondisruptive of the course of life Hume ridiculed as that of the easy philosopher in the first section of the first *Enquiry*. They do not please others immediately, except for those who cultivate shallowness in order to achieve a life free of mental exertion and filled with comfort. The best that can be said in their behalf is that they are unlikely to offend others. I cannot understand how they can be derived from the fundamental right/wrong imagery in the human heart, as they do not engage the heart very much, if at all.

On the other hand, Socrates' qualities also are not immediately agreeable. To many of his interlocutors, they are loathsome, even dangerous. Even to his friends, the agreeable response they garner is not immediate, nor is the response ever superficially pleasurable. The same can be said of those figures from our recent past who challenged injustice, such as Gandhi, King, and Mandela. None of the three is noteworthy for his social niceties, although those useful traits—e.g., courage and strength of mind—redound to their honor just as they frustrate and frustrated their enemies. Love of truth, love of justice—these are not immediately agreeable. They are out of place at a cocktail party. Yet they clearly and ultimately shine more brightly than the agreeable qualities that Hume praises here.

Section IX: Conclusion

Part I

In one sense, this section as a whole may be seen as a gathering up of what has been gained in the previous sections and, at the same time, as a return to the origin of the second *Enquiry*. Hume declares his apparently straightforward result, which

> may justly appear surprising that any man in so late an age, should find it requisite to prove, by elaborate reasoning, that Personal Merit [in two later editions: virtue or personal merit] consists altogether in the possession of mental qualities, *useful* or *agreeable* to the *person himself* or to *others*. (*EPM*, 268)

Hume's surprise is matched by our own—or at least by *my* own. First of all, the second *Enquiry*, unlike its theoretical predecessor, contains nothing that can properly be called "elaborate reasoning." It both proceeds from and returns to an image-bound "premise," and "deduces" the "principles of morality" from this single origin. Secondly and perhaps uniquely, Hume finds the determination of virtue to be an easy task; not a single moral conundrum appears in the second *Enquiry*, and the moral life itself seems to accord with the direct application of the mental qualities to actual cases. And this in the work that Hume claims is incomparably his best!

Another notable difference between the first and second *Enquiries* consists of the place of the schools in relation to ordinary life. Hume's skepticism of the first *Enquiry* holds an honored place in the schools. Though one leaves behind the epistemologically nihilistic results of his arguments in the realm of action, these results demonstrate the limits of our knowledge, which make themselves manifest at every turn. In the case of morals, the schools exercise a harmful influence, and academic philosophers find themselves inferior to human beings in the ordinary course of life when it comes to identifying moral principles.

> [T]he complete delineation or description of merit seems to be performed as naturally as a shadow is cast by the sun, or an image is reflected upon water. If the ground, on which the shadow is cast, be not broken and uneven; nor the surface from which the image is reflected, disturbed or confused; a just figure is immediately presented, without any art or attention. And it seems a reasonable presumption, that systems and hypotheses have perverted our natural understanding, when a theory, so simple and obvious, could so long have escaped the most elaborate examination. (*EPM*, 268–69)

The distinguished Hume scholars of "the schools" today have also been obtuse when dealing with Hume's moral philosophy. They fail to heed the clue that the second *Enquiry* is deemed incomparably the best of his writings by its prolific author, and they fail to note its manifestly distinctive feature, namely its fundamental bond to images, and most particularly images of right and wrong in the human heart. This bond to images, far from being a mere concession to our epistemological limits, binds us as well to the rest of humanity. This bond constitutes Hume's saying that "the humanity of one man is the humanity of every one, and the same object touches this passion in all human creatures" (*EPM*, 273).

Hume wonders why his "simple" view was not apparent in the earliest times "from its own evidence, without any argument or disputation" (*EPM*, 268). That is to say, the useful and pleasing qualities *make themselves manifest directly;* it seems here, in his moral philosophy even more so than in his theoretical account of human perception, Husserl might have found still stronger antecedents to his phenomenology. A more critical moral phenomenology, that is, one in which no phenomena occur uninterpreted, could still be read into Hume as guided by the most minimal exegetical apparatus, that is, one that is framed entirely by the images of right and wrong that dwell in every human breast.

Humean self-evidence does not equal logical self-evidence. The nature of language may suggest but does not assure that, for instance, the quality of benevolence will be useful and/or pleasant, although the word has only positive connotations:

> It is sufficient for our present purpose, if it be allowed, what surely . . . cannot be disputed, that there is *some* benevolence, however small, infused into our bosom; *some* spark of friendship for human kind; *some* particle of the dove kneaded into our frame, along with the elements of the wolf and serpent. (*EPM,* 271; emphasis mine)

Thus, language must connect with the nature of basic human imagery if moral distinctions are to arise. Arguments, if any there may be, are parasitical upon this originary relation. In this Hume calls this sentiment of humanity the "rule of right." That is, the rule is not primarily rational, and it does not command obedience and forbid disobedience but rather elicits "applause or censure" in "every man, or most men" (*EPM,* 272). The sentiment of humanity, again, rules the way beauty rules in Platonic dialogues: by inspiring human beings to recollect and to act in accord with what is best in them.

Part II

Once again, the big surprise concerns how easy it is to discharge our "interested *obligation*" (*EPM,* 278) to the life of virtue:

> The sole trouble which she [i.e., virtue] demands, is that of just calculation, and a steady preference of the greater happiness. And if any austere pretenders approach her, enemies to joy and pleasure, she either rejects them as hypocrites and deceivers; or, if she admit them in her train, they are ranked, however, among the least favoured of her votaries. (*EPM,* 279–80)

Joy and pleasure constitute the realm of laughter-loving *(philommeidēs)* Aphrodite, goddess of love, among whose votaries Hume's aforementioned dove is eminently included. Of what he called the "monkish virtues" (*EPM,* 270), Hume has nothing good to say. Many Hume scholars have helpfully pointed out that at the time of its publication, when religion had a great deal more influence in the moral sphere than it does today, this aspect of the second *Enquiry* found much disfavor and censure. In light of this, I can see why the passages that were found offensive then are passed over as harmless now.[26]

However, I strongly suggest that Hume's breezy call for "just calculation, and a steady preference of the greater happiness" (*EPM,* 279) conceals virtually every difficulty that can be found in a moral theory that details qualities of virtue rather than standards of choice. How, for example—to provide a simple and common American example—does one decide whether to purchase the popular toy of the season, say, a Barbie doll, for one's daughter? Raising the stakes several levels, how does one decide to end heroic life-saving measures for a severely ailing parent? Just calculation and a steady preference for the greatest happiness yields—just do the best you can, in accord with the image of rightness in your heart, under the circumstances.

But is this a weakness, perhaps a severe one, of Hume's moral theory? I say: not at all. As I maintained in *Imagination in Kant's Critique of Practical Reason,* no moral theory can account for all phenomena, nor can it answer every objection. Hume's moral theory is of a piece with his theoretical philosophy in this crucial particular, namely, that we humans do not have access to the original good itself, apart from its image (just as we have no access to original truth, aka first causes, but only of constant conjunctions + imagination). In this, it establishes its kinship with major features of the Platonic dialogues concerning our apprehension of the good only through its images (as in *Republic* VI), and with its oft-iterated orientation toward the beauty of goodness (as in *Philebus* 64e). This is the *human* good that calls to us from our hearts.

Further, since moral language is founded on fundamental imagery, the language of right differs essentially from the language of wrong; this parallels the difference between the language of the greater happiness of humanity from the language of self-love. Thus, moral language itself—often and perhaps usually without argument—draws one toward morality. If one will not hear such language but hears only the other kind, she or he cannot be drawn to morality, either by image or by argument.

The only quality that, in Hume's view, could conceivably present a challenge to the view that virtue is always preferable to vice occurs with respect to justice. It might seem that an unjust person could benefit from his or her injustice, and that (by implication) the just person would be the loser by virtue of his or her justice. Hume has two answers: the first, indicated above, that if the unjust person is deaf to the language of morality, there is no way of engagement. Second, injustice involves an erroneous calculation that fails the test of preferring the greatest long-term happiness. The knave often finds himself tripped up by his own malevolence; or, he sacrifices something far more valuable than his ill-gotten gains. But worse still:

> [T]hey themselves are, in the end, the greatest dupes, and have sacrificed the invaluable enjoyment of a character, with themselves at least, for the acquisition of worthless toys and gewgaws. . . . And in a view to *pleasure*, what comparison between the unbought satisfaction of conversation, society, study, even health and the common beauties of nature, but above all the peaceful reflection on one's own

conduct; What comparison, say I, between these and the feverish, empty amusements of luxury and expense? (*EPM,* 283–84)

One of many scarcely noticed wonders of Plato's *Republic* occurs toward the end of the first book and the toward the beginning of the second, where Socrates indicates that he thought that his exchange with Thrasymachus proved that justice is both intrinsically preferable to injustice, and is beneficial to the just man while its opposite is harmful to his opposite.[27] In other words, the dialogue playfully points to the possibility that it could have received a proper conclusion of sorts far short of its more than three hundred pages.

But Glaucon and Adeimantus are neither convinced nor unconvinced, but would like to hear the customary arguments of the many *(hoi polloi)* answered: justice, they say is a compromise between being thought just but doing perfect injustice (this is best), and being thought unjust but doing perfect justice (this is worst). The very long "addendum" that constitutes nine-tenths of the dialogue is as unnecessary for Socrates in *his* valuation of the just life as it is here for Hume in the second *Enquiry*. Socrates was reported to say of the array of goods in the agora: "Often when he looked at the multitude of wares exposed for sale, he would say to himself, 'How many things I can do without.' "[28] Echoing this, Hume's final sentence reads: "These natural pleasures, indeed, are really without price; both because they are below all price in their attainment, and above it in their enjoyment" (*EPM,* 284).

Chapter III

Hume's Philosophy of Art

The question of taste in aesthetic perception, as indicated earlier, does not arise either expressly or implicitly in the Platonic dialogues. However, the dialogues do address the origin of great art. The contrary both seems to be and is the case in Hume's thought, for which genuine aesthetic discernment is a matter of much importance while the origin of great art seems to interest him not at all. A further difference is manifest in the effect of poetry upon the person. In the Platonic dialogues, poetry is discussed almost exclusively in terms of whether it helps or harms the souls of the people who hear it (reading was not, of course, widespread among the ancients). For Hume, poetry is discussed in terms of how its more or less ingenious presentation of the human sentiments engages those same sentiments in its readers and/or spectators, and the best match of poem to listener is characterized by the innocence of the pleasure it brings. But there are significant crossings here, though of a different kind.

There are also intriguing differences within Humean philosophy between the philosophy of art and the other two branches. For one surprising difference, reason plays a larger *positive* role in his aesthetics than in either the theoretical or moral philosophy. In the former, the arguments of reason result one and all in the ongoing discovery of our ignorance. In the latter, which is guided by the right/wrong imagery of the human heart, reason has little to do other than to concur in the discovery of most of the moral qualities. Only justice and political society tax it, and do so not very heavily. While aesthetic judgment is primarily a matter of sentiment, reason must be actively present. As will be shown, the necessary "sound state" requires it, the art object includes it, and the overall view of the subject entails it.

A difficulty in approaching this work that is common to all philosophies of art from the modern period concerns its suitability for our much more recent age. Hume addresses one such matter when he asserts that philosophers give way to other, better ones in future ages, but poets retain their luster. Here, I disagree—my commitment to Continental philosophy does not allow me to acquiesce to Hume's suggestion that "ARISTOTLE, and PLATO, and EPICURUS, and DESCARTES, may successively yield to each other . . ." (*OST,* 149) There are many resources in Hume's aesthetics for Continental philosophy—indeed, for any philosophy—and in the other thinkers mentioned.

Another arises with respect to what at least seems to be a radically altered artistic landscape beginning in the late nineteenth and early twentieth centuries. Artists themselves have challenged the central tenets of their predecessors in their work. Questions of continuity, of the nature of the work of art (if indeed it has a nature), of art's relation to politics, of the relation of the artist to the work of art she or he creates—these questions, among others, lead me to ask an additional question I will attempt to answer toward the end of this chapter: How is Hume's philosophy of art relevant to a century that has seen the so-called Aristotelian unities and their offspring in the visual and aural arts disappear? How, for example, can the Humean view of art deal with Kafka, Virginia Woolf, Duchamp, Schoenberg, Merce Cunningham, Ornette Coleman, not to mention their even more unorthodox heiresses and heirs and *their* postmodernist descendants—if indeed it can?

A different matter that requires attention, perhaps not unrelated to the latter one, is also raised by Hume's text. I would like to agree with the second part of the sentence cited above, ". . . But TERENCE and VIRGIL maintain an universal, undisputed empire over the minds of men" (*OST,* 149). Earlier, he makes the same claim for Homer. Unless the first two names happen to coincide with that of a current celebrity just as the third coincides with an obtuse cartoon character, there is a strong likelihood that fewer than one percent of Americans would recognize these names and a larger but dwindling minority would recognize them in Europe and in the rest of the world. As to their "maintaining an empire over the minds of men," only a miniscule percentage of that very small group has sufficient command of Greek and Latin to respond to Hume's encomium.

Are there more recent modern works to which we can turn that fulfill Hume's lofty criterion? Perhaps most of Shakespeare; perhaps most of Mozart and Beethoven as well; perhaps also works of Da Vinci and Michelangelo. Whether or not the work of such relatively recent but widely celebrated modern painters might qualify, or that of early-twentieth-century choreographers, seems undecidable. In our era, the visual arts tend to be more accessible. Of Homer, Terence, and Virgil, perhaps we can conditionally admit Hume's praise, that is, *if* classical knowledge were as common among educated people as it *should* be. In any case, Hume is correct that there are clear cases of superiority. These are especially plain when the difference in quality is obvious, for example, when comparing the compositions of Beethoven with those of his contemporary, the violin virtuoso Paganini. Less plain but no less decisive is the superiority of Mozart to the good Salieri, a comparison popularized by the imaginative dramatization in the play and film *Amadeus*.

Hume begins by employing the above as an *elenchus* to the accustomed view that taste is no more than a matter of opinion. Taste among human beings differs widely even within homogeneous groups, and terms of praise for works of art are alike (i.e., elegance, spirit, etc.). "But when critics come to particulars, this seeming unanimity vanishes; and it is found, that they had affixed a very different meaning to their expressions" (*OST*, 134). However, the existence of clear cases, together with the agreement that such cases exist, results in the impossibility of maintaining the accustomed view.[1] Thus, in a one-sentence paragraph Hume writes: "It is natural for us to seek a *Standard of Taste*; a rule by which the various sentiments of men may be reconciled; at least a decision afforded confirming one sentiment, and condemning another" (*OST*, 136).

To those who would defend the accustomed view by asserting that beauty does not exist in things themselves but only in the eye of the beholder, just as preferences for certain taste sensations in food issue only from the predilections of the diner, Hume presents these clear cases as a refutation that convinces:

> Whoever would assert an equality of genius and elegance between OGILBY and MILTON, or BUNYAN and ADDISON, would be thought to defend no less an extravagance, than if he had maintained a mole-hill to be as high as TENERIFFE, or a pond as extensive as the ocean. Though there may be found persons, who give the preference to the former authors; no one pays attention to such a taste . . . (*OST*, 137)

These two English writers, whose work appeared within one hundred years of Hume's life, had not passed the test of time; yet they presented clear cases. Can we replace those British names today with the poetry of rock singer JEWEL and that of ELIZABETH BISHOP, or with JAMES PATTERSON and SAUL BELLOW? I certainly hope so . . . but I am just as certainly mistaken, so distant from us has the standard of taste withdrawn.

At the very least, however, Hume's essay recollects and affirms this standard for us today, and serves as a valuable resource even apart from its other noteworthy features. Perhaps its most striking such feature is the claim that aesthetic standards are firmer and more lasting than either philosophical, moral, or scientific ones. Philosophical standards have always been open to dispute. While moral language seems well-fixed, that is, virtue is always praised and vice is always blamed, this fixity is primarily attributable to the nature of language. The particular qualities and actions that constitute virtue are variable across cultures and history. Natural science features discoveries that improve upon and often supplant their predecessors. But the decidedly preclassical Homer still holds all of its centuries-long recognition for artistic excellence, and new discoveries are always shedding more light on the remarkable epics.[2]

The same source that determines Hume's theoretical and moral philosophies also determines his aesthetic philosophy, in a word, "experience; nor are [the rules of composition] any thing but general observations, concerning what has been universally found to please in all countries and in all ages" (*OST*, 137–38). However, "experience" extends differently in each of the three realms. In the first *Enquiry*, experience extends only to impressions and ideas. When subjected to inquiry, we find that our "knowledge" is restricted to constant conjunction and the belief that such conjunction will continue. In other words, our inquiry into experience ultimately yields only a nonrational psychological connection; in a way, experience as connected perception disappears on the foundation of "experience." In the second *Enquiry*, moral philosophy springs from experience as the common recognition of right/wrong moral imagery in the human heart. Experience is always subject in some way to the sentiment of humanity, in Hume's words. This image-based experience is sustained throughout, and leads to a catalogue of desirable qualities. In neither case does Hume's "experience" require an abundance of sophistication to grasp, although the first *Enquiry* displays unmatched subtlety of argument while the latter offers the most rigorous image-play in modern philosophy.

What is required for genuine aesthetic experience in accord with the standard toward which Hume has so strongly gestured? The most general answer is: a very great deal. On the part of the spectator, every one of these conditions must be met concurrently: (1) it must occur at a proper time and place; (2) the imagination must be suitably disposed; (3) the mind must be perfectly serene; (4) thought must duly recollect what is germane; and (5) proper attention to the object must be paid. "[I]f any of these circumstances be wanting, our experiment will be fallacious, and we shall be unable to judge of the catholic and universal beauty" (*OST*, 139). I am sure that this holds true for me, and I venture to say that it also holds for the vast majority of even those who love art the most, not only that these five conditions have never been met concurrently but that it is a rare and happy occasion indeed when more than two are operative at any one time.

Hume does not himself claim to have achieved this state. It is an experience that requires a mix of exacting discipline and exceptional good fortune to have enjoyed this particular "experience." In this light, it does not surprise when Hume turns immediately to Homer as a model in order to illustrate it. (1) We are at sufficient distance from it in virtually every way to make "now" a proper time and place; (2) when we pick up either epic, it is assumed that our imagination is disposed toward it; (3) this can never be established certainly, but the transport to the ancient Greek language facilitates equanimity of mind; (4) thought recollects the mythical material; and (5) the epic fully engages our attention with respect to its prosodic and rhythmic qualities. That Hume uses an example from a "dead" language is no accident. Anything English, European, Asian, or African is either too close or altogether too distant. As we "all" have access to a language and two poems that are complete in themselves, the Homeric epics are almost uniquely able to provide an occasion for a display of the aforementioned concurrently required qualities. Through them, one can enjoy genuine aesthetic experience.

What happens in cases when the aesthetic experience does not occur, which—one must say—is in almost every case? A sound state in each person consists of the aforementioned collection of qualities. A defective state consists of . . . well . . . everything else! Hume declares "want of delicacy" to be one obvious cause. Once again, he gives a convincing example, a vicarious image—this one from a comic scene in *Don Quixote*—instead of a definition. Sancho Panza relates his hereditary excellence in the discernment of wine quality to a squire with a large nose: one of his ancestors correctly identified a leathern taste and the other a metallic one in a quantity of wine. Though ridiculed by the others present, a key tied to a strip of leather was later found. Therefore, though beauty and deformity belong to sentiment rather than to objects, "it must be allowed, that there are certain qualities in objects which are fitted by nature to produce those particular feelings" (*OST,* 141). Delicacy requires the sensitive apprehension of those qualities that produce those particular feelings:

> Where the organs are so fine as to allow nothing to escape them, and at the same time so exact as to perceive every ingredient in this composition, this we call delicacy of taste, whether we employ these terms in the literal or metaphorical sense. (*OST,* 141)

This quality serves also, as was shown in the second *Enquiry,* as a particularly useful quality, which might even exceed philosophy in the happiness it brings, at least as a result of the pure pleasure it affords. Once again, however, Hume speaks of exceptionally attuned organs, compared to which mine, at least, are painfully discordant though my experiences of art are among my most treasured. When I attend the Pittsburgh Symphony Orchestra, I can never say that my sensibility has missed nothing and has perceived every ingredient. In a live jazz concert, which involves spontaneous improvisation, such delicacy may be impossible in principle. Even when I read and reread a short poem of, for example, Louise Glück or Gwendolyn Brooks, I never feel that all the pieces have somehow come together. While these experiences have brought me the widest and deepest pleasure, I cannot claim delicacy in Hume's sense.

Further tests make the attainment of the already virtually impossible standard of taste still "more virtually impossible." One requires the widest possible experience within a particular species of beauty. Another requires frequent re-experiences of an object of that species in many different lights so as not to be overly influenced by a first or second impression before making one's judgment. Still another requires "comparisons between the several species" for "by comparison alone we fix the epithets of praise or blame, and learn how to assign the due degree of each" (*OST,* 144). Finally, delicacy necessitates freedom from prejudice, the ability to regard oneself apart from all affiliations and enmities as "a man in general." Where this does not occur, the judgment is perverted.

Thus, if one were to meet Hume's requirements set by the standard of taste, one must spend one's entire leisure several times over perfecting one's organs, studying and comparing numberless works of art in every species, and all the while—or first of all?—purifying one's outlook of every taint of prejudice. There is no time to work, certainly no time to write philosophical texts, no time to read them after one has read this text and signed on to the achievement of meeting Hume's standard of taste. All this for a quality that is useful to oneself but one without which a person can live a good moral life? What on earth is going on here? Is Hume serious?

I confess that I am not certain. I will venture to say, however, that the virtual impossibility of achieving the standard is—intentionally or not (and I would wager *something* on the former)—another instance of Hume's playfulness within which the deepest seriousness is concealed, akin to the playfulness of the Platonic dialogues. I say "akin," because the similarity here crosses from Hume's judgment in philosophy of art to Socrates' judgment in his pursuit of wisdom generally. If we stipulate that wisdom in the realm of artistic apprehension consists of meeting the standard of taste, then *no one is wise.*[3] To provide an oversimplified but useful example, suppose a reasonable but monolingual English speaker holds the opinion that, let's say, Homer's *Iliad* lacks poetic merit because its lines don't seem to sing. Tell that person that in order to render a proper judgment, one must be quite conversant in Greek. The person "must conclude, upon the whole, that the fault lies in himself . . ." (*OST,* 142). Extend this example as far as you like, and the most one can say is that there are greater and lesser degrees of delicacy, and that ultimately even the most specialized judge must concede the fallibility of her or his judgment or risk a legacy of folly, for example, by deriding French Impressionism as madness, if indeed there is such a legacy.

Recall Plato's *Apology*: "It is likely that the god is really wise and by his oracle means this: 'human wisdom is of little or no worth'" (23a). Where is the kinship with Hume? It is here: the achievement of the standard of taste, just as the achievement of real wisdom, is closed off to human beings. Yet another playful, perhaps even comic element is this: even supposing one could do the impossible and fulfill every listed criterion, works of art continue to be made, requiring ongoing comparisons which, we may assume, would require ongoing alterations in the tasks required to achieve the standard. What, then, is the outcome? Negatively, we must always be prepared to draw the inference against ourselves when presented with a work that we are for some reason unprepared to judge. At the least, we must say "I don't know."

In this regard, Hume's thought offers a rebirth of Socratic ignorance in aesthetic matters. Is there a person anywhere who can claim Humean "delicacy" with respect to the burgeoning of unprecedented forms of art making? One might object that delicacy is no longer a relevant quality. In response and opposition, this is a mere quarrel about a word, in light of the clear matter of fact that curators make decisions concerning what works deserve to be shown, conductors and chamber groups make decisions on what music deserves to be played and heard, respected literary and poetry organizations award prizes to works that they believe merit them.

I have little doubt, for example, that the much-celebrated Elliott Carter is a superb composer, and have no regret about my compact disc purchases of performances of his music. Nor am I sorry about the hours I spent listening—trying to listen—to his music. Why can't I hear it, enjoy it? Why is it honored and enjoyed by critics and aficionados of avant-garde "classical" music? (1) I lack the required . . . something, and (2) the critics and aficionados do not. This is the best answer I can give. However, I have long loved the music of Ornette Coleman, who only recently achieved official recognition from the established judges,[4] though this music presents formidable barriers to access for many people. However, in this case I have been a steady "comparer" of jazz performances, and so find myself concurring confidently with this recognition of his genius. Again, this confirmation represents only the best I, and the critics, can do at this time. There can be no doubt that the decision to award the Pulitzer Prize was based upon the cultivated sensibility of the judges, call it "delicacy" or call it something along similar lines.

Without providing much in the way of transition (and so strengthening my hunch), Hume goes on to observe that "few are qualified to give judgment on *any* work of art" (*OST,* 147; emphasis mine). He implicitly admits that the actual existence of a single qualified critic of any work of art is not necessary to his argument:

> It is sufficient for our present purpose, if we have proved, that the taste of all individuals is not upon an equal footing, and that some men in general, however difficult to be particularly pitched upon, will be acknowledged by universal sentiment to have a preference above others. (*OST,* 148)

Here are two other crossings back to Platonic philosophy, though along somewhat different lines. The issues do not directly concern images and image-play, but rather trace the general limits of human judgment.

The first concerns the rare or nonexistent judge who has its counterpart in *Republic* V, in the course of Socrates' distinguishing the lovers of sights from the philosophers:

> The lovers of hearing and the lovers of sights, on the one hand, I said surely delight in beautiful *(kalas)* sounds and colors and shapes and all that craft makes from such things, but their thought *(dianoia)* is unable to see and delight in the nature of the beautiful itself.
>
> That, he said, is certainly so.
>
> Wouldn't, on the other hand, those who approach the beautiful itself and see it by itself be rare *(spanioi)*?
>
> Very much so *(kai mala)*. (476b–c)

The lovers of hearing and of sights are said to be asleep though they think they are awake; the only ones who are called "awake" are those who can both distinguish the beautiful itself and beautiful things, and can see how beautiful things participate in beauty itself. The latter are the analogues of Hume's superior judges. Regarding the "very rare" one who can see beauty itself by itself, one finds telling silence. Such a one may not be a human being at all. One who fully measures up to Hume's standard of taste—may we not suspect the same?

The second crossing occurs from Hume's discussion of the task of the true critic, whose superior judgment is always open to challenge:

> Whether any particular person be endowed with good sense and a delicate imagination, free from prejudice, may often be the subject of dispute . . . but that such a character is valuable and estimable,

will be agreed in by all mankind. Where these doubts occur . . . men must produce the best arguments that their invention suggests to them; they must acknowledge a true and decisive standard to exist somewhere, to whit, real existence and matter of fact; and they must have indulgence to such as differ from them in their appeals to this standard. (*OST,* 148)

This passage echoes *Phaedo* 100a–e, cited in the chapter treating the first *Enquiry,* in important respects. Socrates "assumes" or "lays down" *(hupothemenos)* what he judged to be the strongest *(errōmenestaton) logos.* That the beautiful itself by itself exists, this he affirms as the strongest *logos*.[5] Whatever harmonizes *(sumphōnein)* with this "assumption" he will call true, and what does not he will regard as untrue.

For Hume, the matter of fact and real existence of a standard of taste conforms to the Socratic presupposition of "beauty itself in itself, goodness itself in itself," and the like. The repeated and very frequent Socratic recourse to the first person in these lines strongly suggests that Socrates is not claiming anything resembling objective truth; indeed, truth could only be said to occur given the assumption. What makes Socrates' "assumption" strongest, then, is not its truth, but rather its ability to fend off all challengers in the contest of *logoi,* or in most current translations, of "arguments." Hume's "best arguments" occur under the power of the matter of fact/real existence of the standard of taste. This matter of fact/real existence cannot be beheld directly any more than Platonic beauty can. Rather, its acceptance must be granted once the phenomenon of clear cases is granted.

With this measuring of Hume's claim, disputes of taste—at least those of a certain kind—do not admit of a decisive answer. A helpful example may be the mid-nineteenth century vitriolic dispute between music critic Eduard Hanslick, champion of Brahms and Mendelssohn and despiser of Wagner and Liszt, and Richard Pohl, enthusiastic partisan of Wagner and Liszt and antagonist of Brahms and Mendelssohn.[6] Though Hanslick is read more frequently today as a result of his provocative formalism, which admits the aesthetic validity only of purely musical emotions and that rules out what he calls "program music" as well as all music designed to elicit "human" emotions, it can be said that in the actual world of music programming Pohl draws even with his antagonist. Though these two critics certainly showed no "indulgence to such as differ from them in their appeals to this standard" (*OST,* 148), less partisan and passionate music directors and conductors have implicitly indulged each of them.

What are we to make of this comment, offered almost as self-evident, in considering Hume as a Platonic philosopher and Continental ancestor:

> Every work of art has [like all noble works of genius] also a certain end or purpose for which it is calculated; and is to be deemed more or less perfect, as it is more or less fitted to attain this end. The object of eloquence is to persuade, of history to instruct, of poetry to please, by means of the passions and the imagination. (*OST,* 146)

This view resists reinterpretation along either path. Hume never gives a description of what he calls "genius." One cannot be certain whether it points to a creative ability that differs in kind from a high degree of technical facility, or only in degree. The Platonic dialogues, while not having such a word at their disposal, nevertheless clearly point to divine inspiration as its source—or what we would call a qualitative distinction. One of its key features is a kind of madness, as we have seen, and not calculation toward a predetermined end. Similarly, Continental philosophy of art, although discourses on genius are not an important part, clearly acknowledges a gift that is special and peculiar to certain artists such as Cezanne, Van Gogh, Klee, and Kandinsky as visual artists, and Hölderlin, Celan, and Keats as poets.

A far more noteworthy difference emerges in Hume's comment on the object or purpose of poetry. Neither in the Platonic dialogues nor for recent Continental philosophy does poetry have as its goal merely "to please by means of the passions and the imagination" (*OST,* 146), though it *may* have this quality as a second-order effect. In both, the close relation between poetry and *truth* constitutes the crux of the issue, which (accordingly) plays a much larger role. In either the traditional interpretation of Plato that regards poetry as dangerous to the soul, or the newer one that regards poetry in a friendly and complementary way, the determination concerning the connection of poetry to truth is a central concern.

And in one of the most influential strains of Continental philosophy, poetry—great poetry—is one of the preeminent sites at which truth happens. In this strain, established earlier by Martin Heidegger and extended by John Sallis, truth is interpreted as the Greek *alētheia—a-lētheia*—un-forgottenness or un-hiddenness. This is the most originary sense of truth; truth as correspondence or coherence are mere second-order offshoots in which *their* origin conceals itself. Untruth, darkness, and ignorance belong essentially to truth's disclosure. Hölderlin *("Was bleibet aber, stiften die Dichter")*[7] and Stefan George among the Germans and especially Sophocles among the Greeks receive sustained interpretive elucidation. Sallis turns more often of late to Shakespeare and to the so-called (and miscalled) English Romantics.

In other words, what for Hume constituted an admirably useful quality to oneself but an ultimately dispensable one for a moral life or, for that matter, a scientifically informed life in the broadest sense of that term, serves as a mainspring if not a cornerstone of the Platonic dialogues and of contemporary Continental philosophy. I must read this sharp difference from within some major insights of the latter. The sensible/intelligible distinction supposedly has its source in Plato's divided line, but as recent (and, in my opinion) entirely convincing Plato scholarship has shown,[8] this belief emerges both from a badly decontextualized reading of that passage, and even more seriously by presupposing this very distinction as one interprets Plato.

By Hume's time, the sensible/intelligible distinction had inscribed itself into the tradition, in the sense that leading philosophers on both sides of the so-called rationalist/empiricist divide guided their discourses in terms of how each conceived the relation between sensation and reason. It redounds to Hume's credit that he disrupted all previous accounts of this relation in his theoretical philosophy, performing what can be called a thoroughgoing *elenchus* in which he proves the impossibility of determining their connection. The case may be more disputable concerning his moral philosophy, yet I do not see how the fundamental imagery of the human heart can be seen otherwise than as anterior to the sensible/intelligible distinction.[9] Despite Hume's own sensitivity to artistic imagery and to the customary acuteness of his analyses, he does not escape the traditional distinction in his aesthetics, at least in this respect.

However, he certainly ranks as one of our ancestors in the following most significant respect. He does not have the slightest scruple concerning the celebration of *beauty* in its wondrous capacity to shine upon the souls of those who behold it, and at one point links it in a way to reason, from which it is otherwise distinct:

> Not to mention, that the same excellence of faculties which contributes to the improvement of reason, the same clearness of conception, the same exactness of distinction, the same vivacity of apprehension, are essential to the operations of true taste, and are its infallible concomitants. It seldom or never happens, that a man of sense, who has experience in any art, cannot judge of its beauty; and it is no less rare to meet with a man who has a just taste without a sound understanding. (*OST,* 147)

As the large majority of Hume's examples are literary, it scarcely surprises that he notes the requirement of being able to follow a series of propositions in a work of imagination just as is required in following a chain of inferences in the sciences. Add to that the above citation that claims their close affinity in the mind of the person of sound sense, and one might ask: What, then, is the difference after all?

Here, we find another instance of Hume's text working against itself with an unexpected and significant result. It appears that sound understanding and true taste, while aligned in the person of acumen, are nonetheless distinct. Sound understanding refers to the operations of reason, true taste refers to the fineness of sentiment. However, what Hume in the first *Enquiry* calls "sound understanding" has a very limited sense. Strictly speaking, its only positive meaning can be found in relations of ideas. With respect to matters of fact, the person whose understanding is actually sound has full awareness of its profound limits.

Our best insights amount to no more than customs, which are reducible to fictions that repeat themselves such that we must believe that they will continue to occur. No other distinction can be made regarding those fictions and the ones we cannot (and therefore do not) believe. According to sound understanding, the phenomenon we call "cause" is nothing other than constant conjunction and the "new" impression (read: sentiment) that it generates. The unavoidable conclusion—at least so it seems to me (this is surely not Hume's own view)—is that there is no difference in kind at all between the theoretical and the aesthetic experience. Both are fundamentally aesthetic, though the nature of the theoretical does not become apparent until one takes a synoptic view of Hume's first *Enquiry* in its own terms.

In this sense, Hume's thought may be regarded as a challenge to the conventional view concerning C. P. Snow's affirmation of two cultures that differ from one another fundamentally.[10] The "facts on the ground" have changed since that 1959 essay. At that time, the humanities were generally regarded as the home of true intellectuals while scientists, while given credit for the technological developments their work has made possible, were often scorned for their comparative lack of literary sensitivity. Now, the sciences rule when it comes to respect and, which may be a more important measure in this contest, money for grants, laboratories, etc. The humanists find themselves having to defend their relevance.

This distinction and state of affairs describes the current state of academic philosophy as well. Analytic style philosophy, which takes its departure more from the sciences, dominates American and British universities, and makes inroads even into their European counterparts. Continental philosophy, which takes its departure more from art and literature, receives little support by comparison. John McCumber's *Time in the Ditch: American Philosophy and the McCarthy Era*[11] offers the intriguing thesis that American philosophy withdrew from facing the important questions of life and retreated into the safe antiseptic domains of logic and linguistic analysis because its practitioners feared repercussions. The result: philosophy departments shrunk in size as their offerings no longer attracted the vital young.[12] This may be so, but the transition in stature between the cultures had already been well on its way.

It has been said often enough to make it a virtual truism that the massive accumulation of human knowledge since the era of Hume and Kant bears responsibility to the differentiation of the cultures, and to the more general fragmentation and specialization of the academy. In the eighteenth century, it was possible in principle to "know everything," Newton's laws and Euclid's geometry, the sum of classical literature and Renaissance art, the principal moral theories, and the arguments of the great philosophers. To say that one practices philosophy[13] in the academy today says very little: Which orientation? Which thinker(s) are studied? Which problems? Which aspects of thinkers and/or problems? Even if the above questions receive clear answers, one still cannot infer much about the nature of the person's thought as one could during the modern era from Descartes through Kant.

However—and this question strikes me as both rhetorical in the narrow sense and as substantive to the highest degree—is it not at least possible to discern the outline of an underlying unity in both philosophy and across the disciplines when Hume is read as an abiding and challenging contemporary rather than as providing a notably influential moment in philosophy's history? The *Stanford Encyclopedia of Philosophy*, a "house organ" of Anglo-American philosophy, notes both Hume's wide influence and argues that he is an anti-metaphysician par excellence. In neither presentation do we find an account of Hume's philosophy taken as a whole:

> [H]is influence is evident in the moral philosophy and economic writings of his close friend Adam Smith. Hume also awakened Immanuel Kant from his "dogmatic slumbers" and "caused the scales to fall" from Jeremy Bentham's eyes. Charles Darwin counted Hume as a central influence, as did "Darwin's bulldog," Thomas Henry Huxley. The diverse directions in which these writers took what they gleaned from reading Hume reflect not only the richness of their sources but also the wide range of his empiricism. Today, philosophers recognize Hume as a precursor of contemporary cognitive science, as well as one of the most thoroughgoing exponents of philosophical naturalism.[14]

At the beginning of the first *Enquiry*, Hume maintains that we "must cultivate true metaphysics with some care, in order to destroy the false and adulterate" (*EHU,* 12). But when he explains what "true metaphysics" is, it turns out not to be metaphysics at all. Hume is urging nothing less than the total reform of philosophy.[15]

I suggest that such Hume-interpretation underrates and misappropriates his philosophy, notwithstanding the opening accolade calling him "[t]he most important philosopher ever to write in English."[16] Books I, II, and III of Hume's *Treatise* conform in a general way to the traditional triad that includes truth, beauty, and goodness. The two *Enquiries* together with "Of the Standard of Taste" also reenact this triad. What makes Hume a great thinker in *any* language is his stand at the juncture of tradition on one hand, and its overcoming by the exposure of tensions within the tradition that drive it beyond itself. Whether or not he is a naturalist, and how that supposed naturalism fits together with his "empiricism" and "skepticism," seems to me to be at most a second-order concern.

I concur with the decision to call him a skeptic, but only in a quite circumscribed sense. His skepticism in his own terms involves a withholding of judgment with the aim of not transgressing the limits of the human understanding. Thus, it not only recalls Socratic ignorance as indicated earlier but also the Greek *skepsis,* from *skeptomai,* which means merely "to look carefully over," or to "consider well." Hume looks over the tradition with the greatest care, and addresses *its* questions with unprecedented acuteness. The claim that the result of his thought is "not metaphysics at all," and that he is seeking "nothing less than the total reform of philosophy" stands beyond hyperbole; it is simply false.

In order to do justice to Hume's contribution, we must—in my view—look upon it in terms of Nietzsche's monumental history, as a great and unified deed that bears abiding witness to the possibility that great deeds may yet be accomplished. Nietzsche, among our most important ancestors, does not mention Hume often, but when he does so it is nearly always with approval. Nevertheless, it is hardly enough, nor is Husserl's deployment of Hume's account of perception. (The best book of Continental thought on Hume is Gilles Deleuze's *Empiricism and Subjectivity: An Essay on Hume's Theory of Human Nature* [1953], a response to which I wrote at the beginning of this book.) The impetus for this book is, in part, to bring his thought alongside the enormous amount of attention paid to German philosophy in the Continental tradition where it belongs and—except for Kant's massive encounter with it—has occasioned a degree of neglect from which correction we will benefit.

Regarding Hume and the metaphysical tradition, I offer the following: Leibniz's "word 'I,' so full of meaning"[17] remains full of meaning. However, its meaning is transformed theoretically into the famous "bundle of perceptions."

A *bundle* persists, and must persist in order for constant conjunctions to occur at all. Metaphysical self-knowledge has nearly always been a red herring. Its limits were sharply circumscribed in Descartes, who denied clear and distinct knowledge to all matters concerning the body save mathematical extension; also in Leibniz, who affirmed the difficulty of grasping distinct elements; and in Spinoza, for whom a life in accord with reason is lived by very few and only with great difficulty. The "I" in moral and aesthetic philosophy presents no problem at all to Hume. Metaphysics, classically defined, is the science of being as being. In no sense does the "I" lack being for Hume; rather, in the theoretical philosophy, this being must be measured and delimited.

The critique of causality, for me, moves in a different direction, toward description and phenomenology without a concept of cause. But it is difficult to maintain that this is *Hume's* opinion. He continued to employ the concept of cause despite the lack of epistemological justification, and had no scruple concerning the use of natural instinct as its explanatory warrant. Perhaps strangely, it is the previously committed Wolffian, Kant, who recognized that Hume's critique of this single concept required "a total reform of philosophy." He undertook this reform not by abandoning the tradition, but by taking it up as a whole and in accord with its usual divisions. It is my strongest conviction that Hume's powerfully original "customary transition *of the imagination* from one object to its usual attendant" (*EHU,* 75; emphasis mine) leads Kant to his own powerful and abiding new notion of a productive imagination. This notion is renewed and further enhanced in the work of Heidegger and, most recently, Sallis.

One can even find early traces of finite imagination and finite transcendence in Hume's discussion of what he calls "innocent and unavoidable" preferences that "can never reasonably be the object of dispute, because there is no standard by which they can be decided" (*OST,* 150). One's nationality, for example, or the time in which one lives, or—most thought-provoking—one's chronological age, can give rise to preferences among works that are otherwise judged as meeting the standard. Hume writes:

> At twenty, OVID may be the favourite author, HORACE at forty, and perhaps TACITUS at fifty. Vainly would we, in such cases, endeavour to enter into the sentiments of others, and divest ourselves of those propensities which are natural to us. We choose our favourite author as we do our friend, from a conformity of humour and disposition. Mirth or passion, sentiment or reflection; whichever of these most predominates in our temper, it gives us a peculiar sympathy with the writer who resembles us. (*OST,* 150)

In other but doubtlessly accurate terms, as one nears death one's preference—one's need, perhaps?—for different kinds of vicarious imaging undergoes change. In still other words, as the body gradually declines from its prime, there is less desire for the erotic vicarious imagery such as offered by Ovid. In middle age, the imagery of the comforts of bourgeois life is more welcome. Finally, as one reaches the threshold of death—*epi gēraos oudō* (328e) as Socrates has it in *Republic* I—perhaps (following Hume) one seeks the larger picture, given in history rather than poetry, into which one can meaningfully locate one's life. One can therefore speak of a standard that engages both spectator and artwork, but one cannot specify the preference of either the spectator or the artwork, nor can one ultimately match them. The best one can do in this regard is to invoke the standard as establishing certain works as meeting the test of time. With respect to those works, an *elenchus* awaits: if the spectator does not admire these works, then the defect is in *him*.

Hume further bows to finitude in his discussion of "the celebrated controversy concerning ancient and modern learning" (*OST,* 151) that takes place toward the end of his essay. Earlier, he appeared to assert that the proper appraisal of the great classical poets requires looking away from the "false content" of some of their lines while concentrating entirely on the conveyance of sentiment and the pleasure that ensues. Here, he seems to alter this position at least to a degree, admitting that

> [t]he want of humanity and decency, so conspicuous in the characters drawn by several of the ancient poets, even sometimes by HOMER and the GREEK tragedians, diminishes considerably the merit of their noble performances, and gives modern authors an advantage over them. (*OST,* 152)

I disagree immediately and sharply with Hume's "considerably." Quite apart from any content, the matchless music of Homer alone lifts his epics above all of the modern authors available in Hume's time, with arguments possible (but not likely, in my view) only for Shakespeare and Milton in English, and though I do not know their languages, Dante and Cervantes and a few others. Even regarding content, Hume's aesthetics does not include an analogue to the Platonic *huponoia,* or underlying sense. Rather, one must *allow* for more or less straightforward falsehoods or age-related moral defects, that is to say, one must somehow overlook them. When it comes to appraising the matter in terms of ancient and modern *learning,* Hume seems to say, the modern authors clearly prevail. Only a somewhat tortuous distinction between artistic excellence and the incorporation of "learning" into artistic production saves Hume from outright contradiction.

Here, the bouquet goes to the ancients—due to their greater sophistication, no less. The way Homer's "Achilles in Hades" passage yielded two different interpretations—one "negative" and the other "positive"—in two different contexts suffices to settle the contest in favor of the ancient, especially in light of the positive interpretation occurring for the human being who has been liberated from the cave.[18] Two more among others: for the training of the guardians as delineated in *Republic* III, Socrates would ban *Odyssey* X, 444–45, since the city does not need guardians who believe that they would become insubstantial nothings should they be slain:

> [Tiresias] alone has intelligence even after death,
> but the rest of them are flittering shadows. (386d)

However, the *Meno* concludes by recommending this identical passage: there are no teachers, nor will any be found

> unless there is someone among our statesmen who can make another into a statesman. If there were one, he could be said to be among the living what Tiresias was said to be among the dead, namely that "he alone retained his intelligence while the others are flitting shadows." In the same manner such a man would, as far as virtue is concerned, here also be the only true thing compared with shadows. (100a)

Finally, the *Republic* finds Socrates deploring poetic depictions of gods undergoing all kinds of transformations, concerned that the guardians' steadfastness would be compromised by such images. However, he employs the same passage playfully from *Odyssey* XVII, 485 to question the Eleatic Stranger's identity in the *Sophist:*

> For the gods take on all sorts of transformations, appearing as strangers from elsewhere, and thus they range at large through the cities, watching to see which men keep the laws, and which are violent. (216a–b)

In the earlier discussion on women, I noted the distortion—or more neutrally, the alteration—that results from the end of what is outrageously called "paganism" and the onset of Christianity, a change that runs so deeply that even Hume cannot resist it. The playful relation of the Greeks to their gods, which includes making them subject to interpretations of all kinds— even Hermes, the messenger god, the "god" of interpretation, is interpreted in many ways[19]—is a relation that is alien to Hume's age, though Hume himself is always ready to ridicule superstition, aka religion as customarily practiced. His thought also undermines the entrenched sensible/intelligible distinction and its offshoots in a momentous manner.

Thus, he has also left the essay "Of Tragedy" for us, a work on aesthetics that serves only to cement his bond to the distinctions his thought so successfully confounded. For Hume, the skill of the author and/or playwright goes no farther than her or his ability to manipulate the passions of the spectators. Hume praises Shakespeare highly for this skill, and praises the turning point of *Othello* for the intensification the poet achieves by focusing upon the hero's impatience, which only serves to magnify his jealousy.[20] However, Hume also criticizes Shakespeare for "great irregularities, and even absurdities, [that] so frequently disfigure the animated and passionate scenes intermixt with them."[21] He refers to Shakespeare's rudeness and lack of theatrical knowledge, and wonders whether he and his contemporaries overrate him by concentrating too much on his most moving moments.

Though echoing the Aristotelian trope "imitation is always of itself agreeable,"[22] Hume's analysis makes no mention of plot, character, or thought—perhaps presupposing them as prerequisites for any worthy such drama. He does, however, place greater emphasis on Aristotle's less highly regarded elements, called diction, song, and spectacle. In his explanation of the paradoxical pleasure that melancholy scenes often produce in the spectator, he writes:

> The genius required to paint objects in a lively manner, the art employed in collecting all the pathetic circumstances, the judgment displayed in disposing them; the exercise, I say, of these noble talents, together with the force of expression, and beauty of oratorical numbers [*rhythms*], diffuse the highest satisfaction on the audience, and excite the most delightful movements.[23]

Another necessary element of this peculiar enjoyment is the constant awareness—dwelling, however, in the background—that one is watching a *play*, that is, that the events are contrived, that it is false, for example, that a real man named Othello kills a blameless real woman named Desdemona, his wife. To show how this unstated but operative background awareness works, he contrasts any theatrical production with Cicero's 70 BC successful prosecution of Verres on numerous corruption charges with respect to his behavior as a leading official in Sicily. While the audience awareness of the background "unreality" of the play before them makes the spectacle of human misery peculiarly pleasurable, Cicero's "actual" artful and convincing rhetoric in detailing Verres's disgraceful malfeasance[24] before the court did not (and would not) bring pleasure.

When one recasts this example in Hume's own terms from the first *Enquiry*, one finds the perspective altered significantly. The difference between, for instance, a theatrical experience of Shakespeare's *Othello* and Cicero's oration against Verres is one of degree and not one of kind; we have direct experience of neither. Of *Othello* and of theatrical and literary productions generally, we have the constant conjunction of the theatrical framework and of the kinds of works that occur within it, which occasions the background sense of unreality. Of actual orations, we have the belief instilled by habit of their reality. And when we consider the Ciceronian oration from this great chronological distance, we may be forgiven if we take the latter to be a theatrical performance.

The irony concealed in Hume's aesthetics concerns its essential conventionality. While giving an acute and thought-provoking account of the standard of taste and saving the idea of beauty in the course of his analyses, he esteems aesthetic experience far less than he does theoretical or moral experience. Delicacy of taste is the most innocent and the purest pleasure, and so gives the most sublime enjoyment to the one who has it. But it ranks below the pursuit of truth, the one passion that does not admit of excess, and below moral rightness, which suffuses human life with light and worth. One would not go too far wrong in saying that the higher two philosophical aspects concern themselves with questions of the nature of reality, while aesthetics concerns itself with the effect of imitations, "mere images," upon their sapient beholders.

But both the theoretical and moral aspects of his philosophy, when followed through in the very way that he established them, give way to insights—"principles"—that are fundamentally aesthetic. That is to say, as reason recedes, as it must, imagination and images move to center stage and shape everything of real consequence. In other words, Hume's philosophy presents human experience as *art*—except when it comes to art.

However, one phrase offered almost in passing suggests something more and other, though it leaves the general structure intact:

> In like manner, a quick and acute perception of beauty and deformity must be the perfection of our mental taste; nor can a man be satisfied with himself while he suspects that any excellence or blemish in a discourse has passed him unobserved. In this case, *the perfection of the man, and the perfection of the sense of feeling, are found to be united.* (*OST,* 143; emphasis mine)

In the perception of beauty, the human being who is divided into reason and sense (passion or sentiment) finds this division overcome, overtaken by what Continental philosophy has called *ecstasy*.

This "perception," to use Hume's language, overcomes itself as a mere perception. In terms of this passage, we see how delicacy of taste reigns as "the purest, the most durable, and most innocent of all enjoyments" (*EPM,* 209) If a slight adjustment is made such that the experience of beauty *uniquely* unifies a human being and sense or feeling, then this experience differs in kind and cannot properly be listed as one enjoyment among others. Ecstasy in Hume? Yes—and another testament to his Continental philosophy ancestry.

Conclusion

I have endeavored to "have Hume speak 'Humean'" wherever possible. In *An Enquiry Concerning the Human Understanding*, which Hume characterizes as a "mental geography," understanding itself had to give way to imagination as the primary region of the mind. Understanding could not reach any determination concerning the most basic operations of the mind, having to remain mute when asked whether images were copies of their originals, whether they were not copies of their originals, or whether such a question ultimately has meaning at all. Every conjunction that the mind makes depends upon imagination, and the essential so-called causal connection that alone renders our experience useful to us proves to be nothing more than imagination constrained to expect our past constant conjunctions to continue—by virtue of a "new" quasi-impression subsequent to the impressions/ideas upon which his empiricism was founded. Instead of a chain of causes, then, a field of images constitutes what we call "reality," with some of the images conjoined constantly and others not.

Even if we would turn our view away from Hume's more common examples such as the nourishing quality of bread, and toward those that are more likely to escape our notice such as the propensity of certain weeds to grow in distant places, a causal connection can never be established by the understanding. I have tried to show that the word *cause*, which we apply to cases of constant conjunction together with habit by means of imagination proves to be nothing more than a habit itself. Hume's own text establishes his thought as a founding pathway for phenomenology, not a confirmation of the empiricism to which this same text sounds the death knell.

Would Hume—the man who lived from 1711 until 1776—agree with this assessment? Although the question makes no real sense, let us suppose for a moment that his text could answer for him—although phenomenology as we know it was a century and a half from being born. If we suppose this, our answer would have to be negative. His Berkeley-interpretation in the first *Enquiry* reflects his view:

> But that all [Berkeley's] arguments, though otherwise intended, are, in reality, merely sceptical, appears from this, *that they admit of no answer and produce no conviction.* Their only effect is to cause that momentary amazement and irresolution and confusion, which is the result of scepticism. (*EHU,* 155n)

Hume's own skepticism, however, proved far more lasting than *momentary* for Kant, who can be said to have erected the massive critical philosophy as a result of the inspiration provided by Hume's philosophy. However, Hume himself did not seem overly distraught by the result of his researches. It is not only possible but likely, given what we know about his disposition, that the despair he would feign in many of his writings is primarily a *literary* phenomenon, and that the radical skepticism in which his purely theoretical research culminates did not cause one second's delay in the onset of his next game of backgammon. There is no evidence that his question to the "excessive" skeptic concerning the aim of his researches and concerning what he proposes as a result is anything but decisive; further, the advent of natural instinct in place of reason clearly seems sincere.

Can we, then, offer anything analogous to Heidegger's famously daring view in *Kant and the Problem of Metaphysics,* according to which Kant withdrew from his own discovery after having glanced into the abyss opened up by it?[1] While there are certain parallels, especially concerning the centrality of imagination, the likeness should be resisted. Even if we stipulated to the salience of Heidegger's insight, we find little concern with *duty* and with the ruling capacity of reason even in Hume's moral philosophy. For Kant, Hume's thought threatened the entire edifice of rational knowledge, and so demanded an answer if one were possible. Though one can excavate some underlying playfulness in Kant's thought, there is little doubt that his philosophy is both serious and arduous.

By contrast, Hume always seems to delight in the movement of his own mind, and to accept the most incendiary insights to which his principles lead him with a casual serenity that belies their force. He makes apparently effortless transitions from his status as a solitary monster to one as a contestant in a game of backgammon, or from odes to benevolence to apologies for the condemnation of women who lapse even once from the strictest chastity. Baier has characterized Hume's philosophy as particularly genial and nonpunitive, "humane and beneficent."[2] The quality of his writing certainly suggests such an overall judgment, together with the plain textual fact that the exacting of retribution receives virtually no attention. Recall Kant's statement: "Even if a Civil Society resolved to dissolve itself with the consent of all its members . . . the last Murderer lying in the prison ought to be executed before the resolution was carried out; . . . for otherwise [the members of that society] might all be regarded as participators in the murder as a public violation of Justice."³ It would seem difficult to imagine a greater contrast.

Nevertheless, Hume's image- and sentiment-based morality is no more and no less systematic and rigorous than Kant's. Kantian practical reason is always surely bound by the categorical imperative, and the morality of any maxim consists entirely of its explicit or implicit universalizability as measured by that imperative. Although it must be conceded that the primary motive of moral action (i.e., sentiment versus reason) seem entirely opposed, and that the actions and dispositions praised and blamed in each can be quite different, a similarity trumps even these most conspicuous disparities. Speaking in a logical mode, in both systems the inference from fundament to "quality" is *indirect*. Speaking in a more aesthetic manner, in both systems the connections between the ruling "element" (i.e., images of right/wrong in the human heart, the categorical imperative) and the ruled "elements" requires a leap of imagination. Similarly, the leaps from the second-order elements (the moral qualities for Hume, the universalizable maxims for Kant) to specific instances of them requires another such leap.

Much can go awry, given the need for two indirect inferences or two leaps of imagination, even if—as I would maintain—the ruling elements are both unimpeachable despite their difference. I have long and firmly believed (though I have not worked out the practical details) that besides history courses that detail intellectual and/or moral triumphs, others should be taught that exclusively chronicle large-scale blindness and/or stupidity and/or mendacity—and that the same qualities can abound in even the greatest philosophers. (Individuals should likewise write an anti-resume or anti-Curriculum Vitae, detailing all of the failures, rejections, foolish words and deeds, etc.) In his 2002 essay "Race and Racism in the Works of David Hume," Eric Morton cites the following passage from Hume's essay "Of National Characters," which one reads today only with great disgust:

> I am apt to suspect the negroes to be naturally inferior to the whites. There scarcely ever was a civilized nation of that complexion, nor even any individual, eminent either in action or speculation. No ingenious manufactures amongst them, no arts, no sciences. On the other hand, the most rude and barbarous of the whites, such as the ancient GERMANS, the present TARTARS, have still something eminent about them, in their valour, form of government, or some other particular. Such a uniform and constant difference could not

happen, in so many countries and ages, if nature had not made an original distinction between these breeds of men. . . . In JAMAICA, indeed, they talk of one negroe as a man of parts and learning; but it is likely he is admired for slender accomplishments, like a parrot who speaks a few words plainly.[4]

For his part, Kant believed that murder is morally superior to masturbation, and had a choice observation of his own on the racial and sexual divisions within humanity:

Father Labat reports that a Negro carpenter, whom he reproached for haughty treatment toward his wives, answered: "You whites are indeed fools, for first you make great concessions to your wives, and afterward you complain when they drive you mad." And it might be that there were something in this which perhaps deserved to be considered; but in short, this fellow was quite black from head to foot, a clear proof that what he said was stupid.[5]

I respond at once and with all the forcefulness that I can summon that neither example reflects upon either the fundament or the quality under it of either Hume's or Kant's moral philosophy. To the contrary, their moral philosophy—which they articulated but for whatever reason violated in its application—animates our revulsion. Where, Hume, is your vaunted benevolence? Where, Kant, is your principle of humanity? The answer: they are in us, they are our heritage, they enabled us to liberate ourselves from at least some of the defects from which you—towering thinkers as you are—were unable to liberate yourselves. Recalling the Nietzschean anomaly treated briefly in the Introduction, their moral philosophy is a monument—a great deed that assures us that great deeds are still possible for life, but that according to today's best insights, some smashing of idols is in order. Preserve the monuments and keep them intact! There are too few of them. I have no objection if some of their surfaces are a bit marred.

A disciplined reading of Hume reveals that experience slips away from this so-called empiricist. The causal principle that would alone render so-called experience accessible to us is—as a principle—unavailable. Nothing can be *established* by the positing of "nature" and "natural instincts." If we regard the attempt to found the causal principle as a comedy, then the sudden interposition of nature functions as a *deus ex machina* much like the Hermes-guided return to earth of Trygaeus in Aristophanes' *Peace* after the hero's dung beetle was no longer available. By contrast both to Kant's magnificent reading and to this one that merely seeks to locate Hume where he properly belongs in contemporary philosophy, the general history of Hume scholarship—even the best of it—is misguided.

Socratic ignorance, and engagement with images: these define Hume's thought. These solicit—or should solicit—Continental philosophers to show Hume's thought the same deep respect as did Kant. Hume is just as much *our* flesh, bones, and blood.

Notes

Introduction

1. David Hume, *A Treatise of Human Nature,* ed. L. A. Selby-Bigge with revisions by P. H. Niddich (Oxford: Oxford at the Clarendon Press, 1978), (hereafter cited in text as *THN*).

2. Immanuel Kant, *Werke Akademie Textausgabe,* Band IV (Berlin: Walter de Gruyter, 1968), 260.

3. Just to be clear, it is my strong conviction that the issue of previous lives is not the point of the myth in the *Meno*. Rather, Socrates concludes with what we would call a conditional: "[N]othing prevents a man, after recalling one thing only—a process men call learning—discovering everything else for himself, if he is brave and does not tire of the search, for searching and learning are, as a whole, recollection" (81d).

4. Immanuel Kant, *Philosophical Correspondence,* trans. Arnulf Zweig (Chicago: University of Chicago Press, 1967), 72.

5. Ibid., 86.

6. Gottfried Martin, *Kant's Metaphysics and Theory of Science,* trans. P. G. Lucas (Manchester: Manchester University Press, 1955).

7. A particularly fine treatment and worthy of particular praise here since it occurs within an analytic approach is that of Mary Burnwart in *Hume's Imagination* (New York: Peter Lang, 1994), where she writes: "Far from being a frail faculty whose movements are controlled by custom and limited to reproduction and replacement, Hume's imagination is capable of useful acts of construction" (24). As the first chapter will show, among imagination's "useful constructions" is the fiction known as cause and effect.

8. At one point he calls it "a bastard of imagination" (Immanuel Kant, *Prolegomena to any Future Metaphysics,* 257–58)—peculiar!

9. I believe that this notion was nascent, at the very least, in Hume. How else to explain the generation of the "new" impression felt by the mind when it appraises a past constant with the belief that it will continue. It becomes explicit in Kant, where he ascribes synthesis in general to the power of imagination *(Einbildungskraft)*. There is nothing like it in his pre-Humean modern predecessors. Its role in analytic Kant

scholarship, for the most part ranging from minor to nonexistent, is a clear indication of its exegetical licentiousness.

10. J. G. Fichte, *Grundlage der gesamten Wissenschftslehre, als Handschrift für seins Zuhörer* (Hamburg: F. Meiner, 1970), I:218.

11. There is, however, one intriguing mention of Hume by Fichte in a letter to Gottlieb Hufeland of August 3, 1795, shortly after the publication of the *Grundlage*. He wrote, "Recently, moreover, while studying Hume's writings I had a revelation. . . . I realized what Kant actually saw as the purpose of [the *Critique of Pure Reason*] . . . I also realized how from this standpoint he was subsequently driven to go further (in the *Critique of Practical Reason* and especially in the *Critique of Judgment* . . .)." He offers to write on these thoughts for Hufeland's *Literatur-Zeitung*. Alas, nothing on them appeared, and we have no record of a response from Hufeland. See J. G. Fichte, *Early Philosophical Writings,* trans. Daniel Breazeale (Ithaca: Cornell University Press, 1988), 405.

12. F. W. J. Schelling, *Schellings Werke,* ed. Manfred Schröter (München: C. H. Beck, 1959), 362; emphasis in original.

13. Ibid., 342.

14. F. W. J. Schelling, *On the History of Modern Philosophy,* trans. Andrew Bowie (Cambridge: Cambridge University Press, 1994), 97.

15. Bernard Freydberg, *Schelling's Dialogical Freedom Essay* (Albany: State University of New York Press, 2008).

16. G. W. F. Hegel, *Vorlesungen über die Geschichte der Philosophie* (Stuttgart: F. Frommanns Verlag, 1959), 493; my translation.

17. Edmund Husserl, *Shorter Works,* ed. Peter McCormick and Frederick Elliston (South Bend: University of Notre Dame Press, 1981), 26.

18. Edmund Husserl, *Logical Investigations,* Vol. I–II, trans. Dermot Moran (New York: Routledge, 2001), I:406.

19. Edmund Husserl, *The Crisis of European Sciences and Transcendental Phenomenology,* trans. David Carr (Evanston: Northwestern University Press, 1970), 88.

20. David Hume, "Of the Standard of Taste," in *David Hume: Selected Essays,* ed. Stephen Copley and Andrew Edgar (New York: Oxford World Classics, 2008), (hereafter cited in text as *OST*).

21. David Hume, *Enquiries Concerning Human Understanding and Concerning the Principles of Morals*, ed. L. A. Selby-Bigge with revisions by P. H. Niddich (Oxford: Oxford at the Clarendon Press, 1975) (hereafter cited in text as *EHU*).

22. Ibid., (hereafter cited in text as *EPM*).

Deleuze's Hume . . . and Ours

1. For evidence of this neglect, one need go no farther than *Deleuze: A Critical Reader,* ed. Paul Patton (Oxford: Wiley-Blackwell, 1996), where one would surely expect to find something on Deleuze's first book. Alas, twenty-six others receive comment,

but not a word is found on this wonderful first text. Such omissions and mentions only in passing occur all too often in Deleuze scholarship. By contrast, one is disappointed but hardly surprised by the virtually total neglect of this challenging book in traditional Hume scholarship.

2. I consciously avoid the debate over Hume's actual position regarding a philosophical sense of theism or deism. In the most usually understood religious sense, he is an atheist. All else seems to me to be splitting hairs . . . though more may be at stake than I am aware of.

3. Gilles Deleuze, *Empiricism and Subjectivity: An Essay on Hume's Theory of Human Nature*, trans. Constantin V. Boudouris (New York: Columbia University Press, 1993), 24; emphasis mine.

4. *The Cambridge Companion to Hume*, ed. David Fate Norton and Jacqueline Taylor (Cambridge: Cambridge University Press, 1993), 1.

5. Deleuze, *Empiricism and Subjectivity*, op. cit., 133.

6. Ibid., 82.

7. Ibid., 83.

8. Ibid., 84.

Chapter I. Aspects of *An Enquiry Concerning Human Understanding*

1. With a mixture of pain and loathing, I read these words of respected Hume scholar J. A. Passmore in *Hume's Intentions* (New York: Basic Books, 1968), which first appeared in 1953: "But Hume's mind, even at its best, was not of the most disciplined sort. Rigour and consistency were not his strong points, and these are qualities which we ordinarily expect from a great philosopher" (152). These complaints echo those of Selby-Bigge, whose editions we still use. One hardly knows how to respond, but I shall try. Rigor and consistency are indeed qualities we ordinarily expect, but of schoolmarms and schoolmasters. There is not a single acknowledged great philosopher whose works do not possess profound exegetical challenges, and whose basic positions are not open to contest and reinterpretation for that reason.

2. An excellent example is Hume: though Hume himself was a racist and a sexist, the spirit of accuracy he here praises and offers as a benefit of the abstruse philosophy has led to the happy lessening of these evils in most parts of the world.

3. Adam Smith, from a letter to William Strachan, November 9, 1776.

4. Henry G. Liddell, Robert Scott, Henry S. Jones, and Roderick McKenzie, *A Greek-English Lexicon* (Oxford: Oxford University Press, 1996), 44.

5. Aristotle, *Physics*, 3:II, 194b–195a.

6. While criticism of your ideas by your adversaries might cause some discomfort, how much less is that an irritant when compared with uncomprehending praise from your friends! Passmore writes: "If all that can be said in Hume's favor that he showed (even unconsciously, as the legend has it) that the theory of ideas could never give an

account of ordinary perception, this would be a lesson worth teaching, one still not universally taken to heart." Leaving aside his parroting of the "theory of ideas" trope, the failure to acknowledge Hume's frequent and express acknowledgement of our necessary ignorance, rather than his "attack on philosophy," is Hume's main achievement and challenge. Passmore, *Hume's Intentions,* op.cit., 153.

7. See the following edition which contains, "This section, as it stands in Editions K, L, and N, . . .": *David Hume, An Inquiry Concerning Human Understanding,* ed. Charles Hendel (New York: Bobbs-Merrill, 1955), 33. The Niddich edition (see Introduction, note 21, above) excludes this.

8. He calls poetry a species of painting! Annette Baier, commenting upon Hume's use of persuasive language, writes: "Hume performs better as skeptic than as painter, preacher, or rhapsodist." *The Cautious Jealous Virtue: Hume on Justice* (Cambridge: Harvard University Press, 2010), 242. I dare say that this sapient scholar has missed the point of Hume's "painting," which is in service to the express role of imagery in *EPM.*

9. Hume, *An Inquiry Concerning Human Understanding,* ed. Charles Hendel, op. cit., 38; emphasis mine.

10. Heraclitus Fragment 45, in *The Presocratic Philosophers,* ed. G. S. Kirk, J. E. Raven, M. Schofield (Cambridge: Cambridge University Press, 1988), 203.

11. Helen Beebee finds this new impression "very puzzling," and properly so. She studies the relevant scholarship closely and judiciously, and reaches her conclusions cautiously. She holds that some of the problems of Hume's account arise from the fact that Hume does not intend to supply a complete explanation, but rather "to give as complete an explanation as is possible given the restrictions of proper scientific methodology." She seems to accept Noonan's suggestion of the new impression as "a feeling of helplessness or inevitability" (Noonan 1999, 142). She reflects contemporary presuppositions when she speaks of "some complex process in the brain whose nature we cannot discern from the nature of the impression that detects it." Helen Beebee, *Hume on Causation* (New York: Routledge, 2006), 85–86. Once again, there is almost a visceral inability to grant privilege to a productive imagination. Can it be called "lack of imagination," even in the case of very talented scholars?

12. If one takes the blinders of traditional scholarship off and reads the dialogues on their own terms, one finds that Socrates never says that he has a theory of ideas (or a theory of anything, for that matter). Recent Continental Plato scholarship has establish this conclusively, despite its minority position. One awaits others to catch up, no doubt in vain. See, for example, John Sallis, *Being and Logos: Reading the Platonic Dialogues,* Third Edition (Bloomington and Indianapolis: Indiana University Press, 1996). Attend especially to 1–6, and to 402–404. Also, my *Play of the Platonic Dialogues* (New York: Peter Lang, 1997), especially chapters 2 and 3, 23–51.

13. Plato, "Letter II," 314c. Despite the learned disputes, according to which the genuineness of every work of Plato has been disputed at one time or other, I accept this letter. I disagree strongly that it does not accord with other aspects of Platonic thought, as some have maintained.

14. See David Fate Norton, "Hume, Human Nature, and the Foundations of Morality," in *The Cambridge Companion to Hume,* op. cit., 158.

15. Aristotle, *Posterior Analytics,* 1:II, 71b.

Chapter II. Aspects of *An Enquiry Concerning the Principles of Morals*

1. Hume, "On the Immortality of the Soul," in *David Hume: Selected Essays,* op. cit., 327.

2. Michael P. Levine, "Hume on Miracles and Immortality," in *A Companion to Hume,* ed. E. Radcliffe (Malden, MA: Blackwell, 2008), 367.

3. Sallis, *Being and Logos,* op. cit., 22.

4. James T. King is a fine Hume scholar whose insight is hampered by his traditional orientation. He writes: "Moral language in use is the point of departure for the *Enquiry* because it is presupposed in any inquiry regarding morality and because, as a fait accompli readily accessible for examination, it is less nebulous than the problematical impressions and sentiments which figure centrally in *Treatise* III." "The Place of the Language of Morals in Hume's Second Enquiry," in *Hume: A Re-evaluation,* ed. D. Livingston and J. T. King (New York: Fordham University Press, 1976), 357–58. He is correct on the importance of language in the second *Enquiry,* but not about its being the point of departure. Hume could not be clearer in stating that the point of departure for all things moral, including moral language, is the imagery of the human heart.

5. Instead of a response to Socrates' question, he launches an ad hominem attack, blaming Socrates for deliberately confusing otherwise expert people, and for being ugly. He concludes with a thinly veiled threat warning Socrates not to leave Athens and come to Thessaly, Meno's city.

6. The original city is "trusty *(alēthinē polis),*" according to Socrates. Each citizen performs his function for the sake of the city, and justice consists in the need each has of the others. Once the desire for luxuries occurs, guardians must be educated both to secure the luxuries through war but to treat their fellow citizens peacefully. It is called "the feverish city," but it is clearly an organized city and quite far from a state of nature. However, it may be possible to interpret the beginning of Book II as depicting a prepolitical situation that set each against all, leading to justice as a compromise. This, to me, is something of a stretch.

7. I have been surprised by the amount of support given to Hume by feminist scholars. It is common to read the most charitable interpretations of Hume's views, which seem to me to be condescending at best and baldly sexist at worst. I find this admirable and inspiring. However, I cannot help but ask whether the attraction consists of the flexibility of Hume's historical empiricism, which can be reread in terms of current feminist commitments, rather than as a challenge to feminism in any sense. I am not sure. See *Feminist Interpretations of David Hume,* ed. Anne Jaap Jacobsen (University Park: Pennsylvania State University Press, 2000).

8. Eugenio Lecaldano, "Hume's Theory of Justice, or Artificial Virtue," in *A Companion to Hume,* op. cit., has insightful comments on this matter. After reporting on Hume's being rejected for a philosophy chair at Edinburgh because the faculty believed that his views undermined the basic distinction between good and evil, Lecaldano disagrees with this judgment at the normative level but notes: "They did however have the merit of grasping that Hume's theory of justice presented an entirely innovative theory that could be reconciled neither with the traditional conception of

natural rights, nor with the attempt made a century before by Hobbes to derive the validity of just laws from a contract or a pact" (257). He also notes that for Hume, justice arose empirically, according to men's needs, "in an entirely casual manner" (261).

9. Bernard Freydberg, *Imagination in Kant's Critique of Practical Reason* (Bloomington and Indianapolis: Indiana University Press, 2008).

10. Adam Smith, *The Theory of Moral Sentiments* (Oxford: Clarendon Press, 1976), 1.

11. Hesiod, *Homeric hymns, Epic cycle, Homerica,* trans. H. G. Evelyn-White (Cambridge: Harvard University Press, 2002), 22–23, lines 256–62.

12. Soloensis Aratus, *Sky Signs: Aratus' Phaenomena,* trans. Stanley Lombardo (Berkeley: North Atlantic Books, 1983), 123.

13. I say "seems" because at the very least, the parallel between city and soul is problematic. This is apparent as early as 430b–c, where Socrates distinguishes between political courage and another kind, which later becomes the courage of the soul.

14. David Hume, "My Own Life" in *An Inquiry Concerning Human Understanding,* ed. Charles Hendel, op. cit., 6–7.

15. Ibid., 7.

16. See Hume, *Enquiries Concerning Human Understanding and Concerning the Principles of Morals,* op. cit., 207, where he claims that the only justification for the community of women is its usefulness. A textually sensitive and therefore properly playful reading would reveal that the community of women is a comic fiction that is impossible to enact even in principle, just as is its counterpart in Aristophanes' *Assemblywomen.*

17. At the outset of *Republic* V, Socrates asks the poets not to mind their own business, but rather to be serious—this after establishing that justice consists of minding one's own business. The comedian's business is to ridicule what is ridiculous; thus, Socrates is aware of the ridiculous, comic nature of what he is about to propose. The first two "waves" ignore fundamental features of the human condition, namely, our sexual nature (see Freydberg, *The Play of the Platonic Dialogues,* op. cit., 118–22). The third, the philosopher-king, contains an internal self-contradiction: the philosopher always hates the willing lie and refuses to tell one; the king must tell many lies for the sake of the ruled.

18. Jane Duran, "Hume on the Gentler Sex," *Philosophia* 31, no. 3–4: 487.

19. Baier, *The Cautious Jealous Virtue,* op. cit., 211.

20. Ibid., 213.

21. François Fénelon, a Catholic theologian and archbishop, is the author of *Les aventures de Télémaque (The Adventures of Telemachus),* first published in 1699, a prose epic that purports to both fill in gaps in the *Odyssey,* that champions peace, that opposes luxury and empire, and that aims at baing understood by women and children as well as men. It had a significant influence on Rousseau's *Èmile.*

22. However, like any powerful political leader, Augustus had his critics during his own reign and thereafter, and contemporary historians such as Anthony Everitt attempt to give a very favorable but balanced view. See Anthony Everitt, *Augustus: The Life of Rome's First Emperor* (New York: Random House Books, 2006).

23. An alternative to Bloom's translation: . . . *kai eis deon erkhē tō logō.*

24. Homer, *Odyssey*, XI: 489–91.

25. One such interpretation is comic: So that my (outward) beauty might match the outward beauty of the young Agathon. Another would indicate a subtle, playful calling into question of beauty as outward, as if elegant (beautiful) clothing could compensate for the famous homeliness of Socrates.

26. Baier makes this point most convincingly. Of Hume's position that the good is the useful, she writes: "This utilitarian inversion would be offensive to the religious, and surely at least a part of what pleased Hume was precisely what offended, namely, *EPM'S* challenge to his own religious and puritan culture." Baier, *The Cautious Jealous Virtue*, op. cit., 246.

27. See 350e–354a.

28. Diogenes Laertius, *Lives of Eminent Philosophers*, Vols. I–II, trans. R. D. Hicks (Cambridge: Harvard University Press, 2000), I: 154–55.

Chapter III. Hume's Philosophy of Art

1. The main issue of the essay, according to Dabney Townsend, "is not about taste per se. The essay is specifically about the problem of a standard—why one must have some standard to settle disputes and how such a standard can be made consistent with the empirical sentimentalism at the heart of Hume's epistemology." Dabney Townsend, *Hume's Aesthetic Theory* (New York: Routledge, 2001), 180. To solve the problem, Townsend distinguishes what might be called three tiers of aesthetic response: first pleasure, an immediate impression for which no account is required; then beauty, which has no definition and which follows upon pleasure but only in response to certain objects; then finally taste, "which operates in advance of any explanations and principles, either directly in terms of qualities or by extension through rules" (183). One problem with Townsend's interpretation may be merely verbal: Hume calls the Standard of Taste "a rule." If I were to attempt to reconcile Townsend's view with my own, I would say that the standard cannot be stated propositionally but experienced as a ruling image arising from the requirements of delicacy, etc.

2. Milman Parry's work earlier in the twentieth century in which he distinguishes oral from written Greek continues to refresh Homeric scholarship. See *The Making of Homeric Verse: The Collected Papers of Milman Parry*, ed. A. Parry (New York: Oxford University Press, 1987). It has spawned a large number of books based on its most fundamental insight, perhaps most notably Gregory Nagy, *The Best of the Achaeans* (Baltimore: Johns Hopkins University Press, 1979). The latter word has itself generated a great deal of scholarship on performance. Other books of a more traditional nature have also broken new ground and inspired other studies, such as James Redfield, *Nature and Culture in the Iliad: Expanded Edition* (Durham: Duke University Press, 1993). I have attempted to interpret the role of Homer in the Platonic *Dialogues* on several occasions. For a brief overview, see "Homeric Methodos in Plato's Socratic Dialogues" in *Philosophy in Dialogue: Plato's Many Devices*, ed. Gary Alan Scott (Evanston: Northwestern University Press, 2007), 111–29.

3. Timothy M. Costelloe writes: "The standard . . . is an abstraction from the activity itself and presents in propositional form what good taste would consist in were individuals free of the imperfections of their nature." Timothy M. Costelloe, *Aesthetics and Morals in the Philosophy of David Hume* (New York: Routledge, 2007), 16–17.

4. His musical effort *Sound Grammar* (Sound Grammar, 2006), recorded live in Germany in 2005, is the first jazz album to receive a Pulitzer Prize. Like many artists with distinctive styles, Coleman endured much ridicule for his composing, his horn and violin playing, and his general approach to music. Obviously, he had his champions as well.

5. There are others along this line, the *eidē*.

6. The overall view of critic Eduard Hanslick that there is no such thing as an extramusical emotion, and who championed Brahms and denounced Wagner, is captured in the following citations from *On the Beautiful in Music*, trans. Cohen (Indianapolis: Bobbs-Merrill, 1959): "[Music's] nature is specifically musical. By this we mean that the beautiful is not contingent upon nor in need of any subject introduced from without, but that consists wholly of sounds artistically combined" (47). "For the object of these pages, it is enough to denounce emphatically as false Wagner's principle theorem as stated in the first volume of *Oper und Drama*," in which Wagner argued that drama was the end and music the mere means. Hanslick continues: "An opera . . . in which the music is really and truly employed as a medium for dramatic expression is a musical monstrosity" (44). By contrast, Richard Pohl, champion of Wagner and "the music of the future," was "swept off his feet by the passionate ideals of the musical romanticists" "Franz Liszt to Richard Pohl," in Edwin N. Waters, *Studies in Romanticism*, Volume VI, Summer 1967, 193.

7. "What remains, the poet establishes." Friedrich Hölderlin, *Werke und Briefe*, Band 1 (Frankfurt am Main: Insel Verlag, 1969), 196.

8. The best source remains John Sallis, *Being and Logos*, op. cit., for its close reading of the second half of Book VI. See especially 401–55.

9. See pp. 40, 83–84 above.

10. See C. P. Snow, *The Two Cultures: and A Second Look* (Cambridge: Cambridge University Press, 1964).

11. John McCumber, *Time in the Ditch: American Philosophy and the McCarthy Era* (Evanston: Northwestern University Press, 2001).

12. A distinguished colleague and friend who received his philosophy PhD from Princeton some years ago related the following pair of statistics recorded in a recent newsletter from his alma mater. Ranking of the Philosophy Department nationwide: #1. Number of undergraduate majors: 0.

13. I adopt the Kantian proscription against calling oneself a philosopher.

14. William Edward Morris, "David Hume," *Stanford Encyclopedia of Philosophy* (2009), http://plato.stanford.edu/entries/hume/#Rel.

15. Ibid.

16. Ibid.

17. Gottfried Wilhelm Leibniz, *Discourse on Metaphysics; Correspondence with Arnauld; Monadology*, trans. George R. Montgomery (La Salle: Open Court, 1988), 58.

18. See pp. 83–84 above.

19. Homeric hymns to Hermes give special emphasis to his status as messenger between human beings and gods, while acknowledging his other service as lord over all animals and as conductor of souls into Hades. His role as messenger features prominently in Socrates' recollection of Diotima's speech in the *Symposium*. In the Orphic hymns to Hermes, there is no mention of his role as intermediary, but he sings of his role as the god of discourse and of sleep. Further, the Homeric hymns claim that Zeus and Maya parented Hermes; the Orphic hymns attribute this parentage to Dionysus and Aphrodite.

20. Hume, "Of Tragedy," in *David Hume: Selected Essays*, op. cit., 130.

21. Remarks of David Hume on Shakespeare in *The Critical Heritage*, ed. Brian Vickers, Vol. IV: 1753–1765 (London and New York: 1995), 176.

22. Hume, "Of Tragedy," in *David Hume: Selected Essays*, op. cit., 129.

23. Ibid., 128–29.

24. Verres was successfully prosecuted for violations in taxation of wheat farmers, and for fostering false allegations against leading landowners during a war by means of taking their slaves—some of which he killed. See Cicero, *The Verrine Orations*, Vol. 1., trans. L. H. G. Greenwood (Cambridge: Harvard University Press, 1959).

Conclusion

1. Martin Heidegger, *Kant und das Problem der Metaphysik* (Frankfurt am Main: V. Klostermann, 1965), 147–49.

2. Baier, *The Cautious Jealous Virtue*, op. cit., 250.

3. Immanuel Kant, *The Philosophy of Law: An Exposition of the Fundamental Principles of Jurisprudence as the Science of Right*, trans. William Hastie (Union, NJ: Lawbook Exchange, 2002), 198.

4. Note to "Of National Characters" by David Hume as quoted by Eric Morton, "Race and Racism in the Works of David Hume" in *Journal on African Philosophy* 1, no. 1 (2002).

5. Immanuel Kant, "Of National Characteristics, so far as They Depend upon the Distinct Feeling of the Beautiful and Sublime" in *Observations on the Feeling of the Beautiful and the Sublime*, trans. John Goldthwait (Berkeley: University of California Press, 1991), 113.

Bibliography

Aratus, Soloensis. *Sky Signs: Aratus' Phaenomena.* Stanley Lombardo, trans. Berkeley: North Atlantic Books, 1983.
Aristotle. *The Complete Works.* Vol. I-II. Jonathan Barnes, ed. Princeton: Princeton University Press, 1984.
Baier, Annette. *The Cautious Jealous Virtue: Hume on Justice.* Cambridge: Harvard University Press, 2010.
Beebee, Helen. *Hume on Causation.* New York: Routledge, 2006.
Burnwart, Mary. *Hume's Imagination.* New York: Peter Lang, 1994.
Cicero. *The Verrine Orations.* Vol. 1. L. H. G. Greenwood, trans. Cambridge: Harvard University Press, 1959.
Costelloe, Timothy M. *Aesthetics and Morals in the Philosophy of David Hume.* New York: Routledge, 2007.
Deleuze, Gilles. *Empiricism and Subjectivity: An Essay on Hume's Theory of Human Nature.* Constantin V. Boudouris, trans. New York: Columbia University Press, 1993.
Duran, Jane. "Hume on the Gentler Sex." In *Philosophia* 31, no. 3–4: 487.
Everitt, Anthony. *Augustus: The Life of Rome's First Emperor.* New York: Random House Books, 2006.
Fichte, J. G. *Early Philosophical Writings.* Daniel Breazeale, trans. Ithaca: Cornell University Press, 1988.
———. *Grundlage der gesamten Wissenschftslehre, als Handschrift für seins Zuhörer.* Hamburg: F. Meiner, 1970.
Freydberg, Bernard. "Homeric Methodos in Plato's Socratic Dialogues" In *Philosophy in Dialogue: Plato's Many Devices.* Gary Alan Scott, ed. Evanston: Northwestern University Press, 2007.
———. *Imagination in Kant's Critique of Practical Reason.* Bloomington and Indianapolis: Indiana University Press, 2008.
———. *Schelling's Dialogical Freedom Essay.* Albany: State University of New York Press, 2008.
———. *The Play of the Platonic Dialogues.* New York: Peter Lang, 1997.
Hanslick, Eduard. *On the Beautiful in Music.* Gustav Cohen trans. Indianapolis: Bobbs-Merrill, 1959.
Hegel, G. F. W. *Vorlesungen über die Geschichte der Philosophie.* Stuttgart: F. Frommanns Verlag, 1959.

Heidegger, Martin. *Kant und das Problem der Metaphysik*. Frankfurt am Main: V. Klostermann, 1965.
Hesiod. *Homeric hymns, Epic cycle, Homerica*. H. G. Evelyn-White, trans. Cambridge: Harvard University Press, 2002.
Hölderlin, Friedrich. *Werke und Briefe*. Band 1. Frankfurt am Main: Insel Verlag, 1969.
Homer. *Illiad*. Vol. I-II. A. T. Murray, trans. Cambridge MA.: Harvard University Press, 1999.
———. *Odyssey*. Vol. I-II. A. T. Murray, trans. Cambridge MA.: Harvard University Press 1995.
Hume, David. *A Treatise of Human Nature*. L. A. Selby-Bigge, ed., with revisions by P. H. Niddich. Oxford: Oxford at the Clarendon Press, 1978.
———. *An Inquiry Concerning Human Understanding*. Charles Hendel, ed. New York: Bobbs-Merrill, 1955.
———. *Enquiries Concerning Human Understanding and Concerning the Principles of Morals*. L. A. Selby-Bigge, ed., with revisions by P. H. Niddich. Oxford: Oxford at the Clarendon Press, 1975.
———. "My Own Life." In *An Inquiry Concerning Human Understanding*. Charles Hendel, ed. New York: Bobbs-Merrill, 1955.
———. "Of Tragedy." In *David Hume: Selected Essays*. Stephen Copley and Andrew Edgar, eds. New York: Oxford World Classics, 2008.
———. "On the Immortality of the Soul" and "Of the Standard of Taste." In *David Hume: Selected Essays*. Stephen Copley and Andrew Edgar, eds. New York: Oxford World Classics, 2008.
Husserl, Edmund. *Logical Investigations*. Vol. I–II. Dermot Moran, trans. New York: Routledge, 2001.
———. *Shorter Works*. Peter McCormick and Frederick Elliston, eds. South Bend: University of Notre Dame Press, 1981.
———. *The Crisis of European Sciences and Transcendental Phenomenology*. David Carr, trans. Evanston: Northwestern University Press, 1970.
Jacobsen, Anne Jaap, ed. *Feminist Interpretations of David Hume*. University Park: Pennsylvania State University Press, 2000.
Kant, Immanuel. "Of National Characteristics, so far as They Depend upon the Distinct Feeling of the Beautiful and Sublime." In *Observations on the Feeling of the Beautiful and the Sublime*. John Goldthwait, trans. Berkeley: University of California Press, 1991.
———. *Philosophical Correspondence*. Arnulf Zweig, trans. Chicago: University of Chicago Press, 1967.
———. *The Philosophy of Law: An Exposition of the Fundamental Principles of Jurisprudence as the Science of Right*. William Hastie, trans. Union, NJ: Lawbook Exchange, 2002.
———. *Werke Akademie Textausgabe*. Band IV. Berlin: Walter de Gruyter, 1968.
King, James T. "The Place of the Language of Morals in Hume's Second Enquiry." In *Hume: A Re-evaluation*. D. Livingston and J. T. King, eds. New York: Fordham University Press, 1976.
Kirk, G. S., Raven, J. E., and Schofield, M., eds. *The Presocratic Philosophers*. Cambridge: Cambridge University Press, 1988.
Laertius, Diogenes. *Lives of Eminent Philosophers*. Vol. I–II. R. D. Hicks, trans. Cambridge: Harvard University Press, 2000.

Leibniz, G. W. *Discourse on Metaphysics; Correspondence with Arnauld; Monadology.* George R. Montgomery, trans. La Salle: Open Court, 1988.
Lecaldano, Eugenio. "Hume's Theory of Justice, or Artificial Virtue." In *A Companion to Hume.* Elizabeth Radcliffe, ed. Malden, MA: Blackwell, 2008.
Levine, Michael P. "Hume on Miracles and Immortality." In *A Companion to Hume.* Elizabeth Radcliffe, ed. Malden, MA: Blackwell, 2008.
Martin, Gottfried. *Kant's Metaphysics and Theory of Science.* P. G. Lucas, trans. Manchester: Manchester University Press, 1955.
McCumber, John. *Time in the Ditch: American Philosophy and the McCarthy Era.* Evanston: Northwestern University Press, 2001.
Morton, Eric. "Race and Racism in the Works of David Hume." In *Journal on African Philosophy* 1, no. 1 (2002).
Nagy, Gregory. *The Best of the Achaeans.* Baltimore: Johns Hopkins University Press, 1979.
Norton, David Fate, and Jacqueline Taylor eds. *The Cambridge Companion to Hume.* Cambridge: Cambridge University Press, 1993.
———. Norton, David Fate. "Hume, Human Nature, and the Foundations of Morality." In *The Cambridge Companion to Hume.* David Fate Norton and Jacqueline Taylor, eds. Cambridge: Cambridge University Press, 1993.
Parry, Milman. *The Making of Homeric Verse: The Collected Papers of Milman Parry.* A. Parry, ed. New York: Oxford University Press, 1987.
Passmore, J. A. *Hume's Intentions.* New York: Basic Books, 1968.
Patton, Paul, ed. *Deleuze: A Critical Reader.* Oxford: Wiley-Blackwell, 1996.
Plato. *Complete Works.* John M. Cooper, ed. Indianapolis: Hackett Publishing Company, Inc., 1997.
Radcliffe, Elizabeth, ed. *A Companion to Hume.* Malden, MA: Blackwell, 2008.
Redfield, James. *Nature and Culture in the Iliad: Expanded Edition.* Durham: Duke University Press, 1993.
Sallis, John. *Being and Logos: Reading the Platonic Dialogues.* Third Edition. Bloomington and Indianapolis: Indiana University Press, 1996.
Schelling, F. W. J. *On the History of Modern Philosophy.* Andrew Bowie, trans. Cambridge: Cambridge University Press, 1994.
———. *Schelling's Werke, nach der Originalausgabe in neuer Anordung.* Vol. I-VI. Manfred Schröter, ed. München: C. H. Beck, 1959.
Smith, Adam. *The Theory of Moral Sentiments.* Oxford: Clarendon Press, 1976.
Snow, C. P. *The Two Cultures and A Second Look.* Cambridge: Cambridge University Press, 1964.
Townsend, Dabney. *Hume's Aesthetic Theory.* New York: Routledge, 2001.
Vickers, Brian. *The Critical Heritage.* Brian Vickers, ed. Vol. IV: 1753–1765. London and New York: 1995.
Waters, Edwin N. "Franz Liszt to Richard Pohl" In *Studies in Romanticism.* (Boston) 6, no. 4 (Summer, 1967).

Index

abstinence, 67
abstraction, 5, 34
abstruse philosophy, 17–23, 29, 44, 121n2
academic philosophy, 33–35, 43–45
Achilles, 29, 40, 57, 81, 83–84, 109
Act of Succession, 71
Adeimantus, 59–60, 74, 92
aesthetics
   and appeal of utility, 70
   and artistic discernment, 99–100
   and association of ideas, 29
   and chronological age, 107–108
   contrasted with other philosophies, 93–96
   Costelloe on, 126n3
   delicacy of aesthetic standards, 97–99
   and image-play, 56
   requirements for aesthetic experience, 96–97
Agathon, 85–86, 125n25
agreeable qualities
   qualities agreeable to oneself, 79–87
   qualities agreeable to others, 87–88
   and useful qualities, 75–78
Ajax, 79–80
Alcibiades, 24
Alexander the Great, 80
allegory of the cave, 37–39, 40, 83–84
Amadeus (1984), 94
American philosophy, 104–105

analytic philosophy, 104
Anaxagoras, 26
animals, 41–43, 59
Anthropology (Kant), 15
antiquarian history, 51
Aphrodite, 90
apodeixis, 46–47
Apollo, 68
Apology of Socrates (Plato), 20, 23–24, 99
archai, 63
aretē, 57, 77
argument, 46. See also logic and *logos*
Aristophanes, 67, 85–86, 116
Aristotle
   and aesthetic standards, 110
   and appeal of utility, 71, 72
   and evolution of philosophy, 94
   on justice, 66
   and natural philosophy, 31
   and "necessary connexion," 36
   and origin of ideas, 27
   and prejudices, 50
   and unity in the arts, 94
   view of poetry, 84
   and wonder, 13
art. See also aesthetics; *specific art forms*
   and association of ideas, 29–30
   changing nature of art, 94
   and conditions of aesthetic experience, 96–100, 103–104

art *(continued)*
  and Continental philosophy, 102
  and human experience, 111
  and madness, 15
  origins of great art, 93
  purpose of, 102
  and reason, 103
  and Socratic ignorance, 99
  and taste, 7, 95
Assemblywoman (Aristophanes), 67–68, 124n16
association of ideas, 5, 10–13, 28–30
atheism, 9, 121n2
Athens, 67
athlios, 78
Augustus, 82

Bacon, Francis, 71–72
Baier, Annette C., 69–70, 78, 114, 125n26
beauty
  and aesthetic standards, 96–98, 100–101, 103, 106, 110–112, 125n1
  and "necessary connexion," 39
  and taste, 85
  and useful qualities, 77
Beebee, Helen, 122n11
Beethoven, Ludwig van, 94–95
belief
  and doubts concerning understanding, 34
  and the easy philosophy, 23
  and imagination, 3, 11–13
  and madness, 14
  and metaphysics, 20
  and operation of understanding, 30–33
benevolence, 53–58, 116
Bentham, Jeremy, 105
Berkeley, George, 5, 7, 25, 35, 113–114
The Best of the Achaeans (Nagy), 125n2
Boreas/Oreithyia myth, 42
Boyle, Robert, 30–31
Brahms, Johannes, 101, 126n7

British empiricism, 25
Brooks, Gwendolyn, 98
Bruno, Giordano, 19
Burnwart, Mary, 119n7
Bush, George W., 71

Caesar, Julius, 79
The Cambridge Companion to Hume (Norton and Taylor, eds.), 10–11
Carter, Elliot, 99
Cassius, 79
causality
  and aesthetic standards, 104
  and association of ideas, 28–30
  and the Continental tradition, 3–5
  and doubts concerning understanding, 34–35
  and the easy philosophy, 23
  and eidetic cause, 48
  and experience, 116
  and image-play, 63
  and imagination, 113
  and madness, 12–13
  and metaphysics, 9
  and morals, 56
  and natural instinct, 7
  and "necessary connexion," 35–41
  and operation of understanding, 31–33
  and origin of ideas, 26–27
  and passivity of reason, 10
  and Platonic notion of beauty, 48
  and reason of animals, 41–42
  and skepticism, 46–48
Cebes, 26
Celan, Paul, 102
Cervantes, Miguel de, 96–97, 108
Cezanne, Paul, 102
chastity, 67–70
Christianity, 60, 109
chronological age, 107–108
Cicero, 54, 55, 110–111
cities, 59, 61–62, 67
classical knowledge and education, 52, 94

Clio, 53
Coleman, Ornette, 99, 126n4
colonialism, 56, 87
commonsense maxims, 17
contemporary values, 62, 71
contiguity, 5, 10, 13
Continental philosophy
   and Deleuze, 1–8, 9, 13, 15, 106
   and Hume's aesthetics, 93–94, 101–103, 104, 106, 112
   Hume's influence on, 1, 3, 4, 6, 8
   and image-play, 56
   and justice, 61
   and Socratic ignorance, 41
Copernicus, Nicolas, 19
Costelloe, Timothy M., 126n3
courage, 80
creativity, 102
critical history, 51–52
Critique of Judgment (Kant), 120n11
Critique of Practical Reason (Kant), 120n11
Critique of Pure Reason (Kant), 2, 63, 120n11
Cromwell, Oliver, 76

Dante Alighieri, 108
Darius, 80
Darwin, Charles, 105
death, 42, 45
deduction, 53
deism, 121n2
Deleuze: A Critical Reader (Patton), 120n1
Deleuze, Giles
   and Continental philosophy, 1–8, 9, 13, 15, 106
   gaps in Deleuze scholarship, 120n1
   Hume's influence on, 106
   and madness, 12–14
   and passivity of reason, 10–12
Delphic oracle, 20, 42
Demosthenes, 80
Derrida, Jacques, 1, 5

Descartes, René, 7, 19, 94, 107
description, 46, 53
Desdemona, 110
Dialogues on Natural Religion (Hume), 19–20
Dikē, 65–66
Dionysus, 68
Diotima, 86
discretion, 76, 77
distributive justice, 66
divine imagination, 3–4, 7
divine inspiration, 84, 102
divine madness, 13, 24, 72–73
dogmatism, 33
Don Quixote (Cervantes), 96–97
duality, 15
Duran, Jane, 69

easy philosophy, 17, 21–23, 44, 87
education
   and artistic excellence, 108
   and classical knowledge, 52, 94
   and justice-consciousness, 61–62
   Socrates on learning, 119n3
eidetic cause, 48
eidos, 40
Eirēnē, 65
Eleatic Stranger, 109
elenchus, 57, 95, 103, 108
empiricism. *See also* reason and rationalism
   and aesthetic philosophy, 7, 103
   and causality, 113, 116
   Deleuze on, 10–12
   and feminism, 123n7
   and Hume's philosophical method, 52–53
   and Hume's subjectivism, 5
   and Kant, 2
   and madness, 15
   and naturalism, 106
   and origin of ideas, 25
Empiricism and Subjectivity (Deleuze), 1, 6, 9, 11, 13
English language, 22

English Romanticism, 102
An Enquiry Concerning Human Understanding (Hume)
and aesthetic standards, 7, 96, 101, 105–106, 111
and association of ideas, 28–30
and Berkeley, 113–114
and doubts concerning human understanding, 30–33, 33–35
and the easy philosophy, 22, 23
and *Enquiry Concerning the Principles of Morals*, 46–48
and Husserl, 5
and madness, 14–15
and "mental geography," 113
and metaphysics, 20
and "necessary connection," 32–33, 35–41
and origin of ideas, 24–28
and power of imagination, 11
and reason of animals, 41–43
and role of schools, 88–89
and skeptical philosophy, 43–45
and species of philosophy, 17–24
An Enquiry Concerning the Principles of Morals (Hume)
and aesthetic standards, 7, 96, 97
and appeal of utility, 70–74
and benevolence, 53–58
and classical education of readers, 52
conclusion, 88–92
context and structure of, 49–53
and human understanding, 46–48
and justice, 58–66
and moral language, 123n4
and "necessary connexion," 40
and political society, 66–70
prelude to sections VI, VII and VIII, 74–75
on useful and agreeable qualities, 75–78, 79–87, 87–88
Epictetus, 33, 81
Epicurus, 55, 94

epistemology
and causality, 9, 107
and empiricism, 125n1
and Hume's skepticism, 89
and madness, 13
and principles of humanity, 74
and reason, 42
and skepticism, 10–11
Erato, 53
Erōs, birth of, 61
erōs
and appeal of utility, 74
and divine madness, 13, 14
and Platonic notion of beauty, 47
and poetical fictions, 60–61
and political society, 67, 68
erromenestaton, 27
eudaimona, 78
Euterpe, 53
evolution of philosophy, 93–94
exhibition, 53
experience, 12, 37, 98
experimentation, 36–37, 53
experimentum crucis, 71–72

feminism, 69–70, 123n7
Fénelon, François, 80, 124n21
Fichte, Johann von Gottlieb, 3–4, 9–10, 120n11
fictions, 11, 58
fidelity, 67, 68, 76–77
Foundation of the Doctrine of Science (Fichte), 3
French Impressionism, 99
frugality, 76

gender issues, 60–61, 67–70, 124n16. *See also* sexuality and sexism; women
generosity, 54–55
genius, 29
George, Stefan, 102
German philosophy, 9–10, 106
Glaucon, 38, 59–60, 65, 74, 92

Glück, Louise, 98
Golden Age, 65
Gondi, Jean-François-Paul de (Cardinal de Retz), 76
"Good Men's Women: Hume on Chastity and Trust," 69–70
Gorgias (Hume), 78
Graces, 65
Greek language
  and aesthetic standards, 22
  and causality, 27, 38, 63
  and defining nature, 34
  and Homeric epics, 97–98
  Kant's familiarity with, 1–2
  and *logos,* 46
  and magnanimity, 79
  and *Methodos,* 26–27
  oral vs. written, 125n2
  and panegyric, 55
  and Platonic thought, 22, 34
  and reason/sentiment duality, 86–87
  and sense of nature, 31
  and skepticism, 106
  and truth, 102
  and utility, 65
Grundlage der gesamte Wissenschaftslehr (Fichte), 3

Hamlet (Shakespeare), 17–18
Hanslick, Eduard, 101, 126n7
happiness, 22–24, 74, 78, 79
Hegel, Georg Wilhelm Friedrich, 4, 10
Heidegger, Martin, 1, 5, 102, 107, 114
Hera, 67
Heracleia, 72
Heraclitus, 31
Hermes, 109–110, 116
Herodotus, 80
Herz, Markus, 2
Hesiod, 86
Hippocrates, 67
Hobbes, Thomas, 59, 64, 124n8
hodos, 26–27
Hölderlin, Friedrich, 9–10, 102

Homer
  and "Achilles in Hades" speech, 40, 83–84, 109
  and aesthetic standards, 96, 97, 108
  and Fénelon, 80–81
  and Hume's aesthetic philosophy, 29, 94
  and madness, 73
  and oral vs. written Greek, 125n2
  and Plato's view of poetry, 86
  and Socrates, 86
  and utility of poetry, 83–84
honesty, 76–77
Horace, 79, 107
Hōrai , 65
Hufeland, Gottlieb, 120n11
humanities, 104
humanity, 48, 116
human nature
  and benevolence, 54
  and comparison of Hume's *Enquiries,* 46
  and madness, 14–15, 52
  and origin of ideas, 25–26
  and skepticism, 47–48
"Hume on the Gentler Sex" (Duran), 69
Hume's Aesthetic Theory (Townsend), 125n1
Hume's Imagination (Burnwart), 119n7
Hume's Intentions (Passmore), 121n1
"Hume's Theory of Justice, or Artificial Virtue" (Lecaldano), 123n8
huponoia, 108
Husserl, Edmund, 1, 5–6, 89, 106
Hutcheson, Francis, 64
Huxley, Thomas Henry, 105

Idealism, German, 9–10
ideas
  association of, 28–30
  and doubts concerning understanding, 34
  and "necessary connexion," 36–37
  origin of, 24–28

Iliad (Homer), 29, 40
images/imagery. *See also* imagination
  and aesthetic standards, 100, 107–108, 111
  and appeal of utility, 70, 72, 73
  and belief, 3
  and causality, 113
  and contemporary Hume scholarship, 89–90
  "image/original" relations, 38
  image-play, 56, 62
  and influence of Hume's philosophy, 117
  and justice, 61–64, 66
  and moral language, 91, 123n4
  and "necessary connexion," 38–40
  and perception of external objects, 43
  and ruling sentiments, 74
  and the second *Enquiry*, 49, 53
  and use of language, 90
imagination
  and aesthetic standards, 111
  and association of ideas, 11, 28–30
  Beebee on, 122n11
  and belief, 11–13
  Burnwart on, 119n7
  and causality, 113
  and the Continental tradition, 2–3
  Deleuze on, 9
  divine imagination, 3–4
  and "fictions," 59
  influence on Continental philosophy, 8
  and justice, 58–60, 62
  Kant on, 119n9
  and madness, 12, 14, 15
  and natural instinct, 7
  and "necessary connexion," 36–38, 38–39, 40–41
  and passivity of reason, 10–11
  and reason of animals, 41
  and skepticism, 44–45
Imagination in Kant's Critique of Practical Reason (Freydberg), 62, 91
Immanuel Kant, Ontologie und Wissenschaft (Martin), 2
immortality, 42, 50
impressions
  and doubts concerning understanding, 34
  ideas contrasted with, 28
  and imagination, 119n9
  and "necessary connexion," 36–37
  and origin of ideas, 24–25
incest, 67–68
induction, 32–33
inference, 32–33
innocence, 86
instinct, 7
intellect, 38–39, 43–44
international relations, 66–67
Ion (Plato), 13, 72, 83

jazz music, 98–99, 126n4
jealousy, 77–78
judgment, 100–101
justice
  and agreeable vs. useful qualities, 77
  and appeal of utility, 70–71, 71–74
  and benevolence, 55
  forms of, 65
  and Hume's moral theory, 91, 115, 123n8
  and interdependence, 123n6
  justice-consciousness, 61–62
  as moral virtue, 66
  and pragmatism, 18
  and reason, 93
  and the second *Enquiry*, 58–66
  and the social good, 79
  social justice, 50
  Socrates on, 92
  and utility, 63–66
Juvenal, 54

kakia, 57
kallistō, 65
Kandinsky, Wassily, 102

Kant, Immanuel
  Hume's influence on, 1–3, 9–10, 105, 116–117
  and Hume's skepticism, 114–115
  and image-play, 63
  on imagination, 119n9
  on madness, 15
  and operation of understanding, 32
  and Plato scholarship, 59
  and prejudices, 50
  and racism, 116
  Kant and the Problem of Metaphysics (Heidegger), 114
Kant's Metaphysics and Theory of Science (Martin), 2
Keats, John, 102
kinetic empiricism, 11
King, James T., 123n4
Klee, Paul, 102
Krauthammer, Charles, 71

law, 58–59
Lecaldano, Eugenio, 123n8
Lectures on the History of Philosophy (Hegel), 4
Leibniz, Gottfried, 3, 7, 106
Leonardo da Vinci, 94
Les aventures de Télémaque (Fénelon), 124n17
limits of knowledge, 89
linguistics, 105. *See also* Greek language
Liszt, Franz, 101
Locke, John, 5, 7, 25
Logical Investigation (Husserl), 5
logic and *logos*
  and aesthetic standards, 101, 105
  English translation of *logos*, 46
  and method, 27
  and operation of understanding, 32–33
  and poetry, 83
  and skeptical philosophy, 45
Longinus, 79
Lycurgus, 86

Madison, James, 82
madness
  Deleuze on, 12–13
  and effect of poetry, 72–73
  and human nature, 52
  and Hume's empiricism, 6
  and measure, 24
  and the Platonic Dialogues, 13–15
  and skeptical philosophy, 45
magnanimity, 79, 81
The Making of Homeric Verse (Parry), 125n2
marriage, 67
Martin, Gottfried, 2
mathematics, 26
McCumber, John, 104–105
Medea, 80
megalopsychia, 81
memory, 28–30, 32–33
Mendelssohn, Moses, 9, 101
Meno (Plato), 57–58, 109, 119n3
mental geography, 20, 22
Merleau-Ponty, Maurice, 1, 5
metaphysics
  and aesthetic standards, 105–107
  and belief, 20
  and causality, 9
  false metaphysics, 23
  and Kant, 114
  and operation of understanding, 30
  and origin of ideas, 27
  rational metaphysics, 2
  and skepticism, 44
methodos, 26–27
Milton, John, 29, 108
misogyny, 69–70
monumental history, 51–52
morality and moral philosophy
  and agreeable vs. useful qualities, 76–77
  and appeal of utility, 70
  and benevolence, 53–58
  foundations of, 46
  and human nature, 49

morality and moral philosophy *(continued)*
  as human phenomenon, 56
  and Hume's aesthetics, 26
  and images, 7
  and moral language, 123n4
  moral relativism, 4
  motives of moral action, 115
  and nature of justice, 74
  and "necessary connexion," 40
  and operation of understanding, 30–31
  and political society, 66–70
  role of reason in, 93
  and virtue, 57–58, 66, 90–91
More, Thomas, 71
Morton, Eric, 115–116
Mozart, Wolfgang Amadeus, 94
Mugabe, Robert, 59
Muses, 13
music, 45, 53, 58, 97–99, 101, 126n7
mutual shining, 63
"My Own Life" (Hume), 44–45
mythos, 42, 46–47

Nagy, Gregory, 125n2
natural instinct, 7, 27–28, 36–37
Nature and Culture in the Iliad (Redfield), 125
nature and natural philosophy
  and abstruse philosophy, 21–22
  and characterization of Hume's philosophy, 26, 34–35, 37, 41, 105–106
  and Deleuze's *Empiricism and Subjectivity*, 9
  and doubts concerning understanding, 33–34
  and Hume's aesthetic philosophy, 96
  and Hume's skepticism, 106
  and limits of human understanding, 18–19
  and natural rights, 124n8
  and operation of understanding, 30–32
  and phenomenology, 15
  and reason of animals, 41–43

"necessary connection," 32–33, 35–41
Newton, Isaac, 105
Newtonian physics, 30–31
Nichomachean Ethics, 56
Nietzsche, Friedrich, 4–5, 51, 106, 116
Norton, David Fate, 10–11
nuclear family, 60

Obama, Barack, 71
objective truth, 101
Odysseus, 76, 79–80
Odyssey (Homer), 79–80, 109, 124n21
"Of Natural Character" (Hume), 115–116
"Of the Standard of Taste" (Hume), 6, 81, 106
"Of Tragedy" (Hume), 110
On the Beautiful in Music (Hanslick), 126n7
On the Sublime (Longinus), 79
On the Uses and Disadvantages of History for Life (Nietzsche), 51
Oper und Drama (Wagner), 126n7
Othello (Shakespeare), 110–111
Ovid, 107–108

Paganini, Niccolò, 94
paganism, 60, 109
Palin, 82
panegyric, 55, 58, 61
Paradise Lost (Milton), 29
Parmenio, 80
Parry, Milman, 125n2
passion, 72, 73
Passmore, J. A., 121n1, 121n6
Peace (Aristophanes), 116–117
Peloponnesian War, 54
Penia, 61
perception, 40, 43–45, 111–112
Pericles, 54
Peripatetics, 76
Phaedo (Plato), 21, 26, 39, 45, 101
Phaedrus (Plato)
  and appeal of utility, 74
  and beauty, 85

and demonstration of proof, 46–47
and madness, 6, 13, 24
and reason of animals, 42
phasmata, 47
phenomenology, 15, 89, 113–114
Philebus (Plato), 84–85
Philip of Macedon, 80
philosopher-kings, 124n17
phrenes, 44
physics, 30–31
Physics (Aristotle), 27
Plato. *See also* Platonic dialogues
  and aesthetic standards, 100
  on death/immortality, 42
  on effect of poetry, 72
  and evolution of philosophy, 94
  Hume compared with, 22
  and madness, 6
  and natural philosophy, 31
  and origin of ideas, 26
  Platonic notion of beauty, 47–48
  and recollection, 1
  and *ruling images,* 63
  and skeptical philosophy, 45
  and Theory of Ideas, 39, 122n12
  and utility of poetry, 83
  and wonder, 13
Platonic city, 59
Platonic dialogues. *See also specific titles*
  and aesthetic standards, 102, 103
  and divine inspiration of poetry, 84
  and Hume's moral theory, 91
  and Hume's "rule of right," 90
  and madness, 13–15
  on origin of great art, 93
  and playfulness, 52, 61
playfulness of Hume
  and aesthetic standards, 98–99
  and "community of women," 124n16
  and the Greek Gods, 109–110
  and Hume's view of chastity, 68
  Husserl on, 6
  and image-play, 56
  and madness, 14

and the Platonic dialogues, 52, 61
and skeptical philosophy, 44, 114
and Socratic ignorance, 26
and Socratic practice, 20
pleasure, 70–74, 84–86, 90–92, 125n1.
  See also agreeable qualities
Plutarch, 54
poetry
  and aesthetic standards, 93, 98, 102
  and appeal of utility, 72–73
  and association of ideas, 29–30
  and "necessary connexion," 40
  poetical fictions, 58–59, 60
  and qualities agreeable to others, 87
  and useful qualities, 81–87
Pohl, Richard, 126n7
political society, 66–70, 93
Polonius, 17–18
Polybius, 71
Polyphemus, 76
Poros, 61
positivism, 6
posits, 39
power, 61
pragmatism, 18
Praxagora, 67
prejudices, 49–50, 52, 98, 107
Presocratic philosophers, 13
productive imagination, 3
program music, 101
Prolegomena (Kant), 1
proof, 46–47
property, 50, 58
prophecy, 13
Protagoras, 83
Protarchus, 85
Pyrrhonism, 43

"Race and Racism in the Works of
  David Hume" (Morton), 115–116
racism, 49–50, 56, 87, 115–116, 121n2
reason and rationalism
  and aesthetic perception, 93
  and aesthetic philosophy, 7

reason and rationalism *(continued)*
  and aesthetic standards, 103–104, 111–112
  of animals, 41–43
  antirationalism, 4–5
  and happiness, 24
  and human nature, 52
  and limits of human understanding, 18
  and madness, 12, 15
  and morality, 46
  and natural instinct, 114
  and Nietzsche, 4–5
  and operation of understanding, 32
  passivity of reason, 10–12
  and philosophy of imagination, 8
  rational metaphysics, 2
  and sentiment, 86
  and skepticism, 44
  subordination to imagination, 8
rectificatory justice, 66
Redfield, James, 125
reflection, 25
religion, 4–5, 33, 110, 125n25
Republic (Plato)
  and aesthetic standards, 84–85, 100, 108
  and *erōs*, 60–61
  and Homer's "Achilles in Hades" speech, 40, 83–84, 109
  and Hume's moral theory, 91
  and marriage, 67
  and nature of justice, 65–66, 74, 92
  and philosophical fiction, 59
  on poetry, 82, 83
  Socrates' final speech, 55
  and utility, 64–65
rhetoric, 46
Rice, Condoleeza, 71
Roman culture, 80
rules of behavior
  and madness, 14
  and political society, 70
  "rule of right," 90

ruling sentiments, 74

Salieri, Antonio, 94
Sallis, John, 52, 102, 107
Schelling, Friedrich von Josef, 3–4, 10
schizophrenia, 44
Scholasticism, 23, 27
science, 7–8, 18, 19, 26–27, 122n11
Scythians, 80
Second Analogy of Experience (Kant), 32
Second Letter (Plato), 45
seers, 39
Selby-Bigge, L. A., 121n1
self-evidence, 89–90
selfishness, 33, 71
self-love, 79
self-preservation, 59
self-regard, 79
sensation
  and aesthetic standards, 103, 111–112
  and "necessary connexion," 35–36, 38–39
  and operation of understanding, 32
  and origin of ideas, 25
  "sensible region," 38–40
  and skeptical philosophy, 43–45
sentiment, 46, 52, 86
Sextus Empiricus, 55
sexuality and sexism
  and the abstruse philosophy, 121n2
  and challenges of Hume's work, 87
  and feminist support for Hume, 123n7
  and Hume's morality, 56
  and justice, 60–61
  and Kant's moral system, 116
  and political society, 67–70
  and the second *Enquiry*, 49–50
Shakespeare, William, 17–18, 94, 102, 108, 110–111
Silver Age, 65
skepticism and skeptical philosophy
  and comparison of Hume's *Enquiries*, 46–48, 88–89

and doubts concerning understanding, 33–35
and "false metaphysics," 23
and the first *Enquiry*, 43–45
and Kant, 114–115
and naturalism, 106
Norton on, 10–11
Smith, Adam, 21, 64–65, 105
Snow, C. P., 104
social contract, 124n8
social justice, 50–51
social life, 19
social utility, 76–77
social virtues, 54–55, 70
societal goods, 63
Socrates. *See also* Socratic ignorance
and "Achilles in Hades" speech, 83–84, 109
and aesthetic standards, 100, 101
and agreeable vs. useful qualities, 77
and appeal of utility, 71
conviction and execution of, 19
and demonstration of proof, 46–47
and doubts concerning understanding, 33
final speech, 55
and forms of happiness, 23–24
and forms of justice, 65
homeliness of, 125n25
on incest, 67
on learning, 119n3
and magnanimity, 81
and nature of justice, 74–75, 123n6, 124n17
and "necessary connexion," 37–40
and origin of ideas, 26–27
and perceptions of beauty, 85–86
and poetical fictions, 59–60
and poetry, 82–83
and prejudices, 50
and qualities agreeable to others, 87–88
and reason of animals, 42–43
and skepticism, 45, 48
and "theory of ideas," 122n12
and utility of poetry, 83, 84
and virtue, 57
Socratic ignorance
and aesthetic standards, 99
and causality, 28
and doubts concerning understanding, 33–34
and Hume's influence on Continental philosophy, 7–8
and Hume's playfulness, 20
and Hume's skepticism, 106
and influence of Hume's philosophy, 117
and operation of understanding, 30
and reason of animals, 41
Solon, 86
Sophist (Plato), 109
Sophists, 83
Sophocles, 102
soul, 45, 50
Sound Grammar (Coleman), 126n4
specialization, academic, 105
Spinoza, Baruch, 7, 107
Standard of Taste (Hume), 94
Stanford Encyclopedia of Philosophy, 105
Stoics, 33
subjectivism, 5
the sublime, 79
suffering of animals, 59
Sunflowers (Van Gogh), 29
superstition, 20, 22–23, 110
sympathy, 71–72, 79, 87
Symposium (Plato), 24, 68, 74, 85

Tacitus, 107
taste. *See also* aesthetics
and aesthetic perception, 93
Aristotelian view of poetry, 84–85
and association of ideas, 29–30
Costelloe on, 126n3
delicacy of, 97–101, 111–112
and Hume's aesthetic philosophy, 94
and Hume's philosophy of art, 7

taste *(continued)*
  and reason, 103–104
  Townsend on, 125n1
  variations in, 95
technological advances, 8
Telemachus, 81
Terence, 94
Theaetetus (Plato), 14
theatrical performance, 110–111
theism, 121n2
theoretical philosophy, 93
Theory of Ideas, 39, 121n6, 122n12
Thrasymachus, 33, 74, 92
Time in the Ditch: American Philosophy and the McCarthy Era (McCumber), 104–105
Tiresias, 109
touch, sense of, 66
Townsend, Dabney, 125n1
Transcendental Deduction, 2
transcendental psychology, 5
A Treatise of Human Nature (Hume)
  and aesthetic standards, 106
  and Continental philosophy, 1
  and Duran, 69
  and Husserl, 5
  and limits of human understanding, 18–19
  and madness, 14
truth, 25, 40, 76–77, 102
Trygaeus, 116
Typhon, 42

Ulysses, 81

utility
  and agreeable vs. useful qualities, 75–78, 86–87, 89
  appeal of, 70–71, 71–74
  and justice, 63–66, 79
  as moral sense, 64
  and political society, 67
  and qualities agreeable to others, 87

Van Gogh, Vincent, 29, 102
Verres, 110–111
Virgil, 82, 94
virtue
  and appeal of utility, 70
  and application of moral theory, 90–91
  and benevolence, 53–55, 57–58
  and Hume's aesthetic philosophy, 96
  and imagery of morality, 7
  and justice, 63, 66, 91–92
  and morality, 57–58
visions, 11
visual arts, 102. *See also* aesthetics

Wagner, Richard, 101, 126n7
warfare, 59
wealth, 77–78
women, 60–61, 67–70. *See also* sexuality and sexism
wonder, 13

Zeus, 67
Zimbabwe, 59